Arthur Featherstone Marshall

The Comedy of Convocation in the English Church

In Two Scenes

Arthur Featherstone Marshall

The Comedy of Convocation in the English Church
In Two Scenes

ISBN/EAN: 9783744778060

Printed in Europe, USA, Canada, Australia, Japan

Cover: Foto ©Lupo / pixelio.de

More available books at **www.hansebooks.com**

THE COMEDY OF CONVOCATION

IN

THE ENGLISH CHURCH,

IN TWO SCENES:

EDITED BY
ARCHDEACON CHASUBLE, D.D.

THIRTIETH THOUSAND.

"Ἵνα τι γέλοιον εἴπῶ καὶ περὶ γελοίου πράγματος.
"Give me leave to be merry on a merry subject."
S. Greg. Naz.

NEW YORK:
THE CATHOLIC PUBLICATION SOCIETY CO.

TO

THE BISHOPS OF THE PAN-ANGLICAN SYNOD,

These Pages

ARE RESPECTFULLY DEDICATED

BY

THE EDITOR.

DRAMATIS PERSONÆ.

VERY REVEREND DEANS	{ BLUNT. PLIABLE. PRIMITIVE. POMPOUS. CRITICAL. }
VENERABLE ARCHDEACONS	{ JOLLY. THEORY. CHASUBLE }
REVEREND DOCTORS	{ EASY. VIEWY. CANDOUR. }
REVERENDS	{ ATHANASIUS BENEDICT. LAVENDER KIDDS. THE PROLOCUTOR. THE PROFESSOR OF HISTORY. THE PROFESSOR OF THEOLOGY. }

SCENE I.

THE JERUSALEM CHAMBER.

SCENE II.

DR. EASY'S DRAWING-ROOM.

SCENE I.

THE JERUSALEM CHAMBER.

DR. EASY rose to propose the question of which he had given notice at the previous sitting of Convocation:—"Would it be considered heresy in the Church of England to deny the existence of God?" It had occurred to him that he should perhaps adopt a form more convenient for the present debate, if he put the question thus:—"Would a clergyman, openly teaching that there was no God, be liable to suspension?"

ARCHDEACON JOLLY thought not. What the Church of England especially prided herself upon was the breadth of her views. No view could be broader than the one just stated, and therefore none more likely to meet with the sanction of the Privy Council, which, he apprehended, was the real point to be kept in view in the discussion of this interesting question. (Hear, hear.)

DEAN BLUNT concurred in the opinion that Breadth and the Privy Council were kindred ideas. Still, it might be asked, could even the doctrinal elasticity of that tribunal become sufficiently expansive to embrace the enormous hypothesis of his learned friend? He ventured to think that it could. Let it be supposed that some clergyman of the Church of England—say the Archbishop of Canterbury—should publicly teach that there was no

God. The case being brought before the Privy Council, it might be reasonably assumed that that supreme Arbiter of Anglican doctrine would deliver some such judgment as the following:—

> "We find that the Church of England is not opposed to the existence of a God. At the same time, we cannot overlook the fact that the nineteenth Article, in affirming that all churches, even the Apostolic, have erred in matters of faith, obviously implies that the Church of England may err also in the same way. Therefore the Church of England may err in teaching that there is a God. We conclude, that whilst, on the one hand, the Archbishop has taken an extreme or one-sided view of the teaching of the Church; on the other, for the reason assigned, it is undoubtedly open to every clergyman either to believe in or to deny the existence of a God."

ARCHDEACON THEORY would be disposed cordially to approve the judgment which the learned Dean anticipated. He had always maintained that it was the *duty* of every Anglican to doubt the existence of God. (Uproar.) Let him not be misunderstood. Speaking for himself, he had a moral and intellectual conviction that there was a God. He was not disputing the objective truth of the existence of a God: about that he could not suppose that a single member of Convocation could entertain the most transitory doubt. He was speaking only of their duty as members of the Church of England, and not at all of their obligation as Christians; two things which might happen in a particular case to be as wide apart as the poles, and to involve distinct and opposite responsibilities. Now, as members of the Church of England, he believed it was their duty to doubt, not only the existence of God, but also every separate article which the Church of England now taught, or might teach hereafter; and the more emphatically the Church of England appeared to teach, the more imperative was their duty to doubt. For, referring to the ingenious argument which Dean Blunt had put into the mouth of their national oracle, it was clear that the Church of England, in denying her own infallibility, laid all her members under the religious obligation of doubting everything she taught. Fallibility, properly defined, was not simply liability to err, it was *the state of error*. As infallibility is a state of certainty, which does not admit of error; so fallibility is a state of doubt, which does not admit of conviction. Now, the Church of England, in proclaiming her own fallibility, did so with a peremptoriness, which elevated this part of her teaching, and this alone, to the dignity of dogma. For whereas in propounding other Anglican tenets, she so adjusted her definitions of doctrine as to leave the choice of possible and opposite interpretations to the discretion of her members; when speaking of this, the fundamental axiom of her whole theological system, she rose for the moment to the authority of a *Teacher*, and consented to put on the robe of infallibility, in order to promulgate with greater force the dogma of her own liability to error.

He would solicit attention to the logical results of this axiom of the Anglican creed. Where there is no infallibility, there can be nothing certain, as the Church of England wisely intimates, except, of course, the obligation of doubting. Consequently, it is one and the same thing to say that we ought to deny the Church's infallibility, and that we ought to doubt what the Church teaches. Now, the Church of England teaches that there is a God. Therefore it is the duty of every Anglican to doubt the existence of a God. And what is true of this article of belief is true of every other. Thus, if the Church of England appear to teach the necessity of Baptism, at the same time that she loudly declares her own fallibility in judging of that necessity, it was their duty and privilege, (as the Privy Council had recently ruled,) to doubt the necessity of Baptism. And if the Church of England appear to teach that she herself is a true Church, at the same time that she proclaims her own fallibility in judging whether she be a true Church or no, and even adds that the truest Churches have at all times grossly *erred*, it was their duty to doubt that she was a true Church. They had no choice about the matter. It was their *duty* to doubt; and no one who did not doubt every doctrine of his Church could be said to comprehend her nature or to be animated by her spirit. This, then, was his answer to the question before the House: "Would it be heresy in an Anglican to deny the existence of God?" He replied that it might be heresy to *deny* the fact, but that it was the plainest of all duties to *doubt* it.

And here he would hazard one other observation on what he had ventured to call the cardinal doctrine of the Church's fallibility.

It was not uncommon in these days for Anglicans to become Roman Catholics. Did he blame them? As a Protestant he must answer, Yes; as an Anglican, No. He was willing to believe that they were guided in that act mainly by their unconscious respect for the teaching of the English Church. For it was obvious that all who are docile to the teaching of that Church must be supremely devoted to her dogma of fallibility, since that dogma is evidently the most fruitful in its consequences, as well as the most clearly defined, in the whole range of her theology. But it was equally clear that as long as an Anglican remained in the Church of England, he could give no adequate proof of his belief in this essential dogma of her fallibility. He might believe it, or he might not. But once let him *leave* the Church, and by that act he manifested to the world his firm conviction that the Church of England was fallible. Consequently, the highest tribute an Anglican could pay to his own Church was to go out of her, and the best proof he could give of belief in her teaching was to connect himself without loss of time with some other communion.

DR. VIEWY here rose, and said that he had listened with deep interest to the ingenious observations of his learned friend. They were, perhaps, too rigidly scientific, and possibly distasteful to some of their colleagues, but he accepted them as a valuable protest against that narrow and Romanistic theology, which Archdeacon Chasuble, and a few others among his reverend friends, were anxious to introduce into the Church of England. For his own part, he hailed the accession of every new view to religion as evidence both of the legitimate fecundity of their National Church, and of the peculiar privileges of her members. It was her glory to have produced during three successive centuries teachers of every shade and variety of Christian doctrine, and to have survived, by a miracle of vitality, their ceaseless battles and disputes, which would have destroyed a less vigorous community, but which she had always serenely contemplated with maternal pride. No other religious society which had hitherto appeared in the world could make the same proud boast. It was, therefore, with satisfaction that he was about to communicate to the House a view of his own perfectly in harmony with the whole history of the Anglican Church, though differing in some points from the one so ably advocated by Archdeacon Theory. It would be found, however, to provide a still more effective clue out of the labyrinth of Anglican difficulties, a valuable guide, if he might be allowed to say so, to his younger brethren, and a complete answer to the question in debate: " Would it be heresy in the Church of England to deny the existence of God?" (Marks of lively attention.)

As an Anglican clergyman, he had always felt bound to teach whatever the Church of England might be supposed to teach. (Applause.) But as that Church, whether interpreted by her clergy or her formularies, was taunted by her enemies with teaching everything and denying everything at the same time, (or at least with permitting every imaginable creed from transcendental Popery down to the baldest Calvinism,) it became necessary for a young clergyman, who would shelter himself from the possibility of heresy, to centre the whole of his obedience in that one bishop or rector, under whom for the time being he might find himself placed. In other words, since to obey any *two* ecclesiastical authorities at the same moment involved the risk of being pronounced a heretic by either one or the other—because no two clergymen are exactly of the same belief—the only effective safeguard against the possibility of heresy was personal obedience to one clergyman at a time. Let the House observe how admirably the principle he was about to develope conciliated rival claims, while it obviated every difficulty arising from variety of doctrine. He argued, then, that personal obedience, the prime duty of every clergyman, was also the remedy for every evil; and he believed that he had carried out that principle in his own career, in a manner which Convocation would approve.

When first ordained to the office of the Diaconate, from which he had been subsequently elevated to unmerited dignities, he found himself in the diocese of a Low-Church bishop,—he might say a very Low-Church bishop,—so low that any further descent into the regions of a purely negative theology would have left no doctrinal residuum whatever. He at once decided, in virtue of his principle of obedience to authority, to teach his flock the religion of his bishop; which, by careful analysis, he resolved into two articles of belief—the denial of dogma, and the assertion of self. (Dean Pompous audibly whispered "highly unbecoming.") But here he had met with a difficulty at starting; for it happened that his rector was a Puseyite; and that, consequently, in the main, whatever the bishop taught to be true, the rector taught to be false, and whatever the bishop taught to be false, the rector taught to be true. The case, as Convocation knew, was so common in this country, as to form perhaps the rule in a majority of parochial cures. His principle, however, suggested an easy escape from the embarrassing position. He applied it thus: Manifestly more obedience was due to a bishop than to a rector; yet a certain *quantum* of obedience was due to a rector, if only because a bishop had appointed him. It became, so to speak, a question of proportion, rather than of theology, and was soluble, not by the Thirty-Nine Articles, but by the rule of three; and after working it out with religious care, the following commended itself to him as the solution of the problem. He would preach Low-Church doctrines on the Sundays, denying the sacramental view and all its consequences, as the homage of clerical obedience due to the bishop; but he would teach High-Church doctrines during the week, without abating a single tenet, in discharge of the proportionate measure of obedience due to the rector. This practice gave rise, he was bound to admit, to some excitement in the parish, and led to the popular conviction that however excellent his teaching might be in detail, there was a want of unity about it when looked at as a whole. Yet when he explained to his parishioners the purity of the motive which induced the apparent contradictions, and proved to them that his duplex system was designed only to reflect justly and proportionately the two aspects of Christianity exhibited by their bishop and their rector, the whole parish at once applauded the delicacy of his conscience, while it ceased not to question the value of his teaching. And so things went on with tolerable harmony for the space of a year; when, unhappily, both the bishop and the rector died about the same time; the former being quickly replaced by a High-Church bishop, appointed by a friend in the Cabinet, and the latter by a Low-Church rector, nominated by Mr. Simeon's trustees. It now became his duty, in consistency with his principle of obedience to personal authority, to invert the order and proportion of his teaching. He would continue to give the Sundays to the bishop, and the week-days to the rector; but on Sundays he must now be a Puseyite, and on week-days an Evangelical; and this simple inversion, so equitable in itself, and inspired solely by the desire of submitting himself to his superiors, created such discord in the parish, that finally he was entreated, as the only means of restoring peace, to resign his cure of souls. At first he ventured to suggest that either the bishop or the rector should resign instead of himself, since their dissensions, not his disobedience, were the source of all this confusion. But this proposal did not meet with that cordial acquiescence which he had a right to expect from either of the parties concerned. Next, he proposed to submit to the arbitration of competent divines, some such problem as the following:—"Given the value of certain Puseyite doctrines, with their Evangelical contraries, to find a mean Christianity;" and he bound himself to accept the resultant as his future standard of orthodoxy. But the arbitrators, after sitting for several days, (during which they were principally occupied in unavailing attempts to convert one another,) abandoned the task in despair; alleging that there was nothing sufficiently definite in either value to admit of their finding a mean.

Hard pressed in this emergency, but more than ever solicitous to sustain the great principle of his ecclesiastical life, he had recourse to a totally new idea. It so happened that the bishop who had ordained him by Letters Dismissory from his own diocesan was neither High-Church nor Low, but of the Moderate or Broad-Church school, and chiefly remarkable for the zeal with which he warned his candidates for orders against "extremes." None of these amiable young Levites could call to mind that his lordship, who was of noble birth, had ever addressed to them any injunction more apostolic than this: "*avoid extremes.*" He therefore begged that he might be permitted to transfer his obedience to that bishop from whom he had originally received what a modern writer had playfully called the "divine commission *not* to teach." This would enable him, while faithful to the obligation of clerical obedience, to take up an independent position in his own parish; and so to preach henceforth, in a quiet and gentlemanly way, against both his bishop and his rector, thus avoiding all invidious distinctions. Unhappily, each fresh attempt at conciliation was less successful than the last; and he was just on the point of resigning his curacy in despair, when a valued counsellor, their distinguished friend and colleague, Dr. Easy, conveyed to him an opportune suggestion. That popular divine, who had risen *pari passu* with himself to the highest summits of their Zion, advised him to promise both bishop and rector, as a final effort to preserve obedience unimpaired, that he would in future abstain from preaching *any* particular kind of Christianity, or from approaching any doctrine to which anybody could object on any ground whatever—a method, Dr. Easy assured him, which was adopted by a large number of amiable and well-bred clergymen in the Church of England. Not averse himself to any arrangement which might meet with the approval of authorities, he embodied this idea in a fourth proposal to both bishop and rector, who were pleased to accept it with decent cordiality, though without any show of enthusiasm. And from that day forward, triumphing in his sovereign principle of obedience to personal authority, he flattered himself, that not the faintest trace of any positive doctrine could be found in any part of his teaching.

Now, applying this history of an incident in his own career to the general question before the House: "Would it be heresy in the Church of England to deny the existence of God?" he thought he had sufficiently proved that it need not necessarily be so. For if heresy, as the etymology of the word implies, consist in the *choice* of one's own creed, as opposed to the submission of the will to authority, it becomes evident that they who always obey can never be guilty of heresy. Assuming that any particular bishop or rector should deny the existence of God, and that the Privy Council should justify him in so doing; granting, further, that obedience to his own bishop or rector is the first duty of a curate,—because in the Church of England there is not, as in the Church of Rome, any supreme or universal authority to obey,—it follows that a curate can only be guilty of heresy when he is guilty of disobedience. Otherwise a curate might set himself up as judge of heresy over his own bishop,—a spectacle they not unfrequently witnessed,—thus making it the bishop's duty to be taught by the curate, instead of the curate's duty to obey the bishop. The mind recoiled from so disastrous a preversion. Such, then, was his own view of the question before the House; and he should, therefore, give his vote in favor of the opinion, that, in the Church of England, it might be *conditionally,* but could not be *necessarily,* heresy to deny the existence of God.

DEAN PLIABLE concurred in the main with the principle

of the learned divine who had just resumed his seat, that obedience to authority was the first duty of a clergyman; but he utterly differed from him in his application of the principle, which appeared to him to be equally servile and injudicious. That principle he conceived to be most effectually carried out, not by abject submission to this bishop or that, this rector or that,—which might be both possible and convenient if in the Church of England, as in the Church of Rome, every bishop and every rector taught the same Christianity,—but in the larger and nobler aim of faithfully representing at one and the same time *all* the Christianities taught by all the bishops and all the rectors of the Church of England. In other words, since every one confessed that it was impossible to teach a uniform theology in the Church of England, whose highest tribunal had ruled that her clergy might teach *either* of two opposite doctrines—and therefore both alternately—he was brought to the conviction that the only course open to Anglicans solicitous about theoretical unity was to profess at the same moment every doctrine held within their communion, and all their contradictories. (Great uproar: a well-known preacher was heard to exclaim—"He would convert us into ecclesiastical acrobats.") Dean Pliable, however, continued: He was not to be diverted by unseemly interruptions, and should calmly pursue the tenor of his argument. There might, indeed, be clergymen, timid lovers of compromise, who quailed before what he was willing to call the painful necessity of their position, and shrank from that large and bold, but only practical view of Anglican unity of which he was the advocate. His own mind was of a less effeminate type. He would add, that, throughout his long ministerial career, which had not been wholly unfruitful, —(partial cheers)—he had not ceased to maintain this view, which he would take leave to call the only honest, logical, and consistent view in the present condition of their great national community. When inducted to his first curacy, under circumstances identical with those described by Dr. Viewy, he resolved to expound the principle in question in all its integrity. Mounting the pulpit on that interesting occasion of a first discourse,—a moment which he doubted not was present to the memory of most of his colleagues, —and taking for his text the sublime words of St. Paul, "One Lord, One Faith, One Baptism," he delivered to an agricultural but anxious and attentive congregation, the following summa of that Anglican theology which it would be henceforth his duty to unfold to them. He had reason to know that his sermon had been warmly approved by many of the more eminent clergy on both sides of the Atlantic, and that at least one Anglican bishop was accustomed to propose it to candidates for orders as a model which they would do well to imitate.

"ONE LORD, ONE FAITH, ONE BAPTISM."

"These words, my brethren, on a first impression, may seem to you to imply an undue restriction on the liberties of the Protestant mind. Listen, however, while I explain to you the Anglican Theology as taught by your bishop, your rector, and myself; and you will confess that whatever St. Paul may have designed by Christian unity, the Church of England has put an interpretation on his words which relieves them of all suspicion of intolerance.

I. In regard of baptism, which the great Apostle calls one of the "foundations" of Christianity, you may believe with your rector, who, as you are aware, was appointed over you by your bishop, that *without* baptism it is impossible to enter the kingdom of heaven, and that it is always accompanied by the new birth.

(2.) At the same time, you are evidently at liberty to consider it with your bishop, to whom both your rector and myself have promised a faithful obedience, to be a mere form or ceremony, having no connexion whatever with the new birth, and therefore wholly unnecessary to salvation.

(3.) Finally, you may agree with me, your approved and licensed curate, as regards Christian doctrine in general and baptism in particular, that extremes are always to be avoided, and that on the whole it is better to accept baptism as a customary and not disedifying ceremony, extremely well-adapted to little children, but without entertaining any morbid prejudice as to its possible effects on the soul.

II. With respect to the Lord's Supper, you can hold with your rector that the effect of consecration in the element is to produce *some* kind of real presence, which, however, does not admit of any attempt at definition, and which is commonly expounded with the greatest vagueness by those who profess to hold it with the greatest precision. You may also believe with your rector—if you are capable of the effort which such an opinion implies—that what you perceive in the chancel is not a table but an altar, and that when you come to church your real object is to assist at "the celebration of the adorable mysteries."

(2.) Should these views commend themselves to your attention, they will doubtless be rendered all the more attractive by the fact that they are sternly prohibited by your own bishop; who requires you, as you would be saved, to maintain that in the Church of England there is no such thing as an altar; that the above doctrine is mere Popery; that the sacrifice of the Mass is a blasphemous fable and a dangerous deceit, plainly repugnant, as the Articles affirm, to the Word of God; that consecration produces no change whatever on the elements; that the object of covering the elements with the hands, as the rubric commands, is to *prevent* any change being wrought upon them; that the doctrine of the real presence is a gross superstition, to protest against which the Church of England was expressly created in the sixteenth century: in short, that the High-Church doctrine, as your bishop justly remarks, is "rank Popery," while the Low-Church doctrine, as your rector judiciously observes, is "filthy Calvinism."

(3.) There yet remains, however, another view of the subject, which approves itself to many of the clergy, and which may be warmly recommended as being most in harmony with the formularies and the practice of our Church: that the change in the elements, if any, and whatever it be, is solely due to the recipient himself, who, of his own free will and power, consecrates, or declines to consecrate, just as he pleases; the faith of the communicant, and not the act of the minister, determining the character of the elements; or, to put this view more simply, say that the Lord's Supper is a monthly or quarterly devotion, in which serious persons receive a little bread and wine, neither with nor without any particular real presence.

III. As to the doctrine of the Visible Church, what it is, and who belongs to it, you are again provided with three distinct and perfectly opposite views upon the point; while in regard of this, as every other doctrine, the Church of England carries delicate forbearance so far as to refrain from intruding upon you any assistance in making your choice between them. Have you Catholic tendencies? Then you may insist with your rector that without the Apostolic succession there can be no true priesthood; and that outside the three branches of the Catholic Church, the Roman, the Greek, and the Anglican, there can be no true sacraments, no valid ministry, and only a perilously vague and cloudy chance of salvation.

(2.) But you may also enjoy the privilege of believing with your bishop, that in the pure reformed Christianity there is no such thing as a priesthood, which is a Popish figment to be utterly reprobated of all faithful people; and that to belong to the Church means simply to reject dogma, abhor Popery, and have an inward assurance that you are one of the elect.

(3.) But if neither of these views should happen to coincide exactly with your own impressions on the subject, you may consider— and this perhaps is a more rational belief than either of the other two—that the Church is what each person thinks it to be, and that, therefore, everybody belongs to it who says he does; whilst with regard to ordination, as retained in our reformed communion, it is probably more scriptural, and certainly more gentlemanly, than the not being ordained, giving to our admirable clergy a certain caste and position in society, which, as everybody perceives, is totally wanting to dissenting ministers.

IV. And now I approach the painful question of the Roman Church. With your rector you may tenderly breathe forth the prayer, "Would to God we were one with our sweet sister Rome, through whom we derive our orders, our creeds, and all our Catholicity." You may even assert with him, and a good many other clergymen of his particular school, that they alone are faithful members of the English Church, who claim to hold all Roman doctrine, and openly advocate union both with Rome and Moscow, though, probably, with as much expectation of obtaining the one as the other.

(2.) If, however, you should find yourselves unable to take up this position, which must certainly be rather a constrained and trying attitude for Protestants, you may, with your bishop, fervently exclaim: "Away with the Church of Rome from the face of the earth; for she is the Beast of the Apocalypse, the great Babylon, several Antichrists, the pit of damnable idolatry, and generally the implacable foe of truth, progress, liberty, morality, virtue, decency, and enlightenment."

(3.) But, my brethren, how far more edifying will be your moderation and charity, if, in this particular, as in every other, you observe the golden rule, which is, "to approve every form of belief except a definite one;" remembering that it is open to you, as it is to your clergy, to believe what you like about the Roman Church, as about the Church of England; and that it is therefore scarcely prudent to censure the belief of Roman Catholics, which you may one day use your undoubted right to exchange for your own.

V. Next, as to Confession and Absolution. Though probably most of you have never heard of either, and cannot therefore be expected to take a deep interest in the subject, still it is my duty as your spiritual guide to explain to you the relations in which you stand toward them. First, then, you may hold with your rector that confession to God's priest is a most blessed and tender provision for afflicted and penitent souls, a divinely-appointed remedy for spiritual wounds, which the Saviour of the world bequeathed to sinners from His cross.

(2.) If, however, you should adopt this view, you will perhaps be disposed to wonder that your Church allowed so wholesome a practice to fall into abeyance for three hundred years, and you may use the liberty your Church permits you, to adopt the more consistent opinion of your excellent bishop: that confession is a disgusting and immoral practice, a vile and insidious cheat of priest-craft, by which people sin more easily, and priests get souls into their power, but which, happily, fell into merited disuse in our own reformed land, because Englishmen are much too pure, great, and good to retain so detestable an usage.

(3.) But truer still, and far more worthy of your common sense, will be the deep conviction, that Confession is not popular in this country, chiefly on two accounts; first, because even the highest churchmen have a lurking suspicion that their priests are wanting in the requisite powers to absolve, having neither faculties to hear confessions, nor training for so difficult and delicate an office; and, secondly, because it may be that Englishmen detect a certain incongruity in confessing their sins to a reverend gentleman who is on nuptial terms with the wife of his bosom, and has several daughters to marry."

He, Dean Pliable, had advanced thus far in his discourse, purposing to complete in the same manner the whole cycle of Anglican theology, when the clerk coming up the pulpit stairs put a slip of paper into his hand from the rector, on which were written the two words, "Pray desist." In compliance with this request, he hurriedly finished his discourse; and, on the following Monday morning, his rector, calling him into his library, counselled him in the kindest manner to seek another curacy. It was in consequence of this event, destined to have results not contemplated by the rector, that he was shortly after named incumbent of a well-known proprietary chapel in the western regions of the metropolis, to which he was followed by a deputation from his rector's flock bearing in their hands a costly testimonial, in the form of an appropriate piece of plate.

And now, it only remained for him to explain, in conclusion, why he had entered into these details, and what was their bearing upon the solemn question before the House: "Would it be considered heresy in the Church of England to deny the existence of God?" What he had already said would enable Convocation to anticipate his reply. The meditations of a long life, directed especially towards the character, the principles, and the practice of the English Church, obliged him to say candidly, that if an Anglican bishop, backed by the Privy Council, should reply to the question in the negative, and instruct his clergy that, at least as a matter of discipline, it would *not* be heresy, such a decision could only be regarded as the honest and logical completion of a system of theology, which having already determined in manifold ways that there is no such thing as positive Christian truth, must consistently admit that there need not be necessarily a personal Christian God.

A few minutes of painful silence here ensued, when—

DEAN CRITICAL inquired, with a touch of irony in his voice and manner—"Could any of his reverend friends undertake to inform him what *was* the authority of the Church of England?" Hitherto the debate had gone only to show what it was *not*. Dr. Theory had maintained that there was no such thing. Dr. Viewy and Dean Pliable had each of them proved that it did not reside in the bishops and clergy, unless indeed it might be supposed to exist in equal measure in every one of them; but as they were unhappily in direct opposition to one another on many fundamental doctrines, this was equivalent to saying that *no* authority to decide Christian doctrine existed in the Church of England. If there really were any such authority, Convocation could hardly be more usefully employed than in defining its nature and fixing its limits.

ARCHDEACON JOLLY observed, without rising from his seat —"What say you to the Archbishop of Canterbury?" (Some laughter, which was immediately suppressed.)

DEAN CRITICAL reminded the venerable archdeacon that the Archbishop of Canterbury was not alluded to in their formularies in any such character, and feared it must be said, without disrespect, that he had no more power to determine a disputed point of doctrine than his amiable lady, whose hospitality many of them had enjoyed. It was a lamentable fact that his Grace had no more authority over the people of England, nor over a single individual out of his own household, than . . . (a voice exclaimed, "the King of the Sandwich Islands," a suggestion which was greeted with mingled applause and disapprobation.)

ARCHDEACON JOLLY: Well, then, Her Majesty the Queen, whom the Church admits to be "supreme" in all causes, spiritual as well as temporal?

DEAN CRITICAL could not forget that Her Majesty, in whom they recognized a model of every Christian virtue, frequented indifferently Presbyterian meeting-houses and the churches of their own communion. If, therefore, as the law appeared to admit, the authority of the Anglican Church resided in her royal person, it followed that the Westminster Confession and the Thirty-Nine Articles were equally true, and that every Anglican was also a Presbyterian.

ARCHDEACON JOLLY: "How about the Privy Council? If it be the ultimate judge of doctrine, must it not be the authority for which you are seeking?"

DEAN CRITICAL thought not, because in fact the sum of its decisions amounted to this—that the Church of England taught nothing, and denied nothing, which was equivalent to saying that she believed nothing. A tribunal which decided in every case of disputed doctrine, as the Privy Council invariably did, that both the plaintiff and defendant were right, was a judicial curiosity that could hardly be said to afford the litigant parties much assistance in bringing their cause to an issue. The Privy Council might be an authority *over* the Church of England, whose decisions the latter was obliged to receive; but no one could seriously maintain that it was an authority to which any Anglican, of whatever party in the Church, professed to submit his conscience in matters of faith.

ARCHDEACON JOLLY: "Will you accept Convocation as your authority?" (Loud laughter, with cries of "Shame" from Dean Pompous.)

DEAN CRITICAL regretted that he could not accept Convocation in the character of an Anglican Holy See; because, to say nothing of the general feeling of the country, and the malicious comments of the public press, which appeared to treat them with derision, and talked of their "dancing round a May-pole," his own observation of the proceedings of that Assembly dissuaded him from any such view. Much experience had brought him to the sorrowful conviction that Convocation was only a clerical debating club, of which every member took himself for the Pope, and the Church for his pupil.

ARCHDEACON JOLLY: "Might it be permitted to suggest the formularies?"

DEAN CRITICAL: So supple and elastic in their nature as to

be sworn to with equal facility both by those who claim to "hold all Roman doctrine" and those who protest against it.

ARCHDEACON JOLLY: "Well, there are still the Thirty-Nine Articles."

DEAN CRITICAL: Thirty-Nine *opinions*, one of which declares of all the others, that they are human and fallible.

ARCHDEACON JOLLY did not know that he could offer any further suggestion, but, at least, one of the Articles declared, "the Church *hath* authority in matters of faith."

DEAN CRITICAL was not unmindful of the fact, which had always appeared to him to be a device of the framers to express this idea: "We admit that the Church we are forming *has* no authority, but we recognise that if it were a Church, it *would* have authority." For it should be observed that while they said, "the Church *hath* authority," they at the same time enjoined the clergy not to believe a single word she taught them, unless they found their own interpretation of the Scriptures to agree with hers! Thus, they made the Church of England say to all her members: "If you should accidentally be *right* in your interpretation of the Bible, put that down to *me*, for I am the Church which teaches you; but if, which is far more probable, you should be wrong, put that down to yourself, for I have warned you to believe in nothing which you cannot prove for yourself out of the Bible." ("Hear, hear," from the Rev. Lavender Kidds.)

DEAN CRITICAL—(after contemplating Mr. Kidds through his eye-glass)—continued: He would gladly and thankfully find in the Articles, if it were possible to do so, both an authority and a summary of positive doctrine. But how stood the case? The very Articles which affirm that the Church *hath* authority were expressly written to prove that it hath *not*. Even the preface to the Articles was a manifest attempt at throwing dust in the eyes of the public, and making them believe the exact contrary of what the writers knew to be true. Thus it stated that the Articles were composed to "*avoid* diversities of opinion," whereas it was notorious to the whole world that they were so framed as to *include* diversities of opinion. It said further, that "His Majesty would not endure any varying or departing from them," which did not seem to imply much confidence in their power to keep their own ground, and made his Majesty the real but somewhat inefficient guardian of their contradictory propositions. It said again that "no man should put *his own* sense or comment upon their meaning." Really the drollest requirement! For, as it had been proved from the beginning, and more than ever in their own times, that they were capable of many and opposite interpretations, whose sense should a man put upon them unless he put his own?

THE PROFESSOR OF HISTORY: Dean Critical was no doubt aware, that, according to Dr. Pusey, the true light by which to interpret the Articles was to be borrowed from the canons of the Council of Trent.

DEAN CRITICAL did not see why, if every man might choose his own sense, Dr. Pusey might not choose his own interpreter, though he could have wished he had made a better choice. But he was surprised that Dr. Pusey did not detect the inconsistency of making the Roman Church the interpreter of Articles which were not only directed against herself, but which formed the very charter of a rival community, whose creation they expressly justified by setting forth the errors and even the blasphemies of Roman theology. It was really too much to make the Roman Church at once the interpreter of charges brought against her, and the judge of the parties who brought them.

THE PROFESSOR OF HISTORY: It was not the less true that they must find a judge *somewhere*, otherwise the Articles were so much waste paper. Could they not be made to interpret themselves?

DEAN CRITICAL thought that their friend Dr. Theory had sufficiently demonstrated—first, that there was really nothing to interpret; and, secondly, that even if there were, there was nobody authorised to interpret it. He had been painfully struck by the observation of his learned friend, that a Church proclaiming its own fallibility could neither teach any definite doctrine, nor enforce it on the conscience of its members. The Articles were his best witness to the truth of the assertion. Thus, one of them decreed that the Church *hath* authority, whilst it not only enjoined all Anglicans *not* to obey it, but even instructed them how to evade obedience by pleading their own interpretation of the Bible. Another of them announced that even General Councils were incurably addicted to "erring," as though the erring propensities of Councils were to be taken for proof that the Church *hath* authority, instead of for proof that it could not possibly have any. Yet General Councils were certainly regarded by the authors of the Prayer-Book as the highest authority after the Bible. How, then, was it possible to extract any plea for authority of any kind from the Articles? "I am sorry for you, General Councils, *but you err*," is the remarkable form of obedience to authority suggested by the Anglican Church to her clergy! He must repeat, that there was something at once trivial and impertinent in a Church declaring that it *hath* authority, whilst in the same breath it commanded its disciples *not* to obey that authority. The authors of the Articles seem themselves to have felt the absurdity; for in the nineteenth Article they made the Church of England say virtually, "I *cannot* teach you, nevertheless obey;" whilst in the twentieth Article, they made her declare, "I *can* teach you, nevertheless do *not* obey." It repented him (Dean Critical), and it was a relief both to his conscience and to his intellect to make the avowal, that he had thrice sworn to the Thirty-Nine; though perhaps, as an undergraduate, the act was partly excused by the fact of his never having read them, and, as a beneficed clergyman, by the circumstance that the law was too strong for him. He appealed to all who respected truth and integrity, and did not consider themselves mere ecclesiastical machines to be wound up and set in motion by an Act of Parliament, whether it was possible to imagine a more grotesque form of impiety and dishonesty than the swearing to the divine truth of what one swears at the same time to be human? He would remind the House of the caustic and ingenious rebuke of the Count de Maistre, than which nothing, he conceived, was ever more conspicuously merited: "In the very same moment, with the very same pen, with the same ink, and upon the same paper, the Church of England declares a dogma, and declares that she has no right to declare it. I hope," added the Count, "that in the endless catalogue of human inconsistencies, this will always hold one of the first places." And he (Dean Critical) must venture to add his own hope to that of the Count, that the swearing, no matter how often, to the divine truth of what one swears to be human, must be far too puerile an act to be reckoned a sin.

DR. EASY here rose to express his regret that, up to the present time, no progress whatever had been made towards that important discovery which was the object of their present discussion.

(He was proceeding to confess his cordial agreement with Dean Critical, as a clergyman and a gentleman, that subscription to the Articles was something very like an insult to a liberal and cultivated mind, when he was suddenly interrupted by the Rev. Lavender Kidds, who appeared not to notice that any one was occupying the House.)

The REV. LAVENDER KIDDS, (who seemed much excited, and rose amidst cries of "Order, order," and considerable laughter), observed that he now assisted for the first time at the Assembly of Convocation, and had been deeply shocked by the unscriptural tone of the discussion. (Suppressed merriment.) For his part, he gloried in the Thirty-Nine Articles of their pure and reformed Church, and especially in their noble testimony to the grand truth that the religion of Protestants was the "Bible, the whole Bible, and nothing but the Bible." This was the true "Authority" of vital Christians, and he cared for no other. This was the simple and grand lesson of those venerable formularies which had been tnat day so grievously undervalued and calumniated. Really, it seemed to him to be preposterous in any Protestant assembly to talk so much of "Church-authority." Authority, indeed! Who wanted it? And if they had it, who would obey it? Certainly no member of that House with whom he had the happiness of being acquainted,—(laughter and ironical cheers,)—least of all the High-Church party, who had recently been forming a society to protect themselves *against* their bishops. (Renewed disapprobation.) He contended that their forefathers had done without authority, and had wisely regarded it as a mark of the Beast. He was for the Bible and the Bible only. Perish the Articles, and the Church itself—no, his zeal was perhaps carrying him too far. What he meant to say was—in fact, he wished to observe—as long as they had the Word they wanted nothing else. He knew, ndeed, that Dean Primitive and Archdeacon Chasuble preferred

Authority to Scripture—as long, that was, as they could keep the former entirely in their own hands; but he had invariably remarked that they refused to their bishops and superiors the obedience they required from their curates and parishioners. But Englishmen, he felt convinced, were not to be cajoled by a spurious Popery; and if they must renounce their liberty, it would not be to those who used that liberty themselves to resist the very Church they copied in everything but their obedience. (General cries of "Enough, enough," amid which Mr. Kidds resumed his seat, with the air of one who had delivered a solemn and suitable protest.)

DEAN BLUNT regretted that Mr. Kidds had so abruptly terminated his discourse. He respected every conscientious opinion, but feared that Mr. Kidds had failed to grasp the real point under discussion. The reverend gentleman need only reflect that the interpretation of Scripture texts was even still more various and incongruous than that of the Articles, in order to convince himself that if authority were wanted to determine the one, it was at least as essential to expound the other.

It was curious that Mr. Kidds did not perceive that everybody had the Bible as well as himself, but that everybody drew a different Christianity out of it. From the Socinian, who denies the divinity of the Lord who bought him, up to the Puseyite, who believes in everything Catholic except in the Catholic Church—all were Bible Christians. But this was only another way of saying that Bible Christianity is, of all fallacies, the most transparent; the fallacy consisting in this, that no professedly Bible Christian ever really takes the Bible for his authority; what he always takes is his own interpretation of the Bible, that is, *himself*. So that, "the Bible, and the Bible only," meant really "*my* interpretation of the Bible, and not yours." Hence, the Bible and self were synonymous terms in the mouth of the Bible Christian. For example (continued Dean Blunt, with a candour which appeared to startle Convocation), if Mr. Kidds take a text of the Bible as meaning one thing, and I take the same text as meaning exactly the contrary, it is obvious that neither Mr. Kidds nor myself takes the Bible for our authority: what we take is ourselves: but as nobody has sufficient sincerity to say openly, "my only authority is myself," therefore, Mr. Kidds calls his opinions "the Bible," and I call Mr. Kidds' opinions "unscriptural."

He (Dean Blunt) would only detain the House to suggest to Mr. Kidds the answer he must give to the question proposed by Dr. Easy. Assuming Mr. Kidds' theory—that a man's conviction of the truth is the same with truth itself; in other words, that heresy *becomes* the truth to every one who *thinks* he finds it in the Bible—the real solution of Dr. Easy's question was as follows: "Let a man be sure that the Bible teaches that there is a God, and then he is a heretic if he deny it; but let him have the smallest doubt upon the point, and then he is a heretic if he assert it."

DEAN PRIMITIVE was unwilling that the observations of Mr. Kidds should pass without any other reply than Dean Blunt had thought fit to give them. He had spent thirty years of his life in combating the errors of that party in the Church to which Mr. Kidds belonged, and he hoped to continue the same holy warfare to the end. He was aware that the so-called Evangelicals insisted upon the *plainness* of Scripture, and were accustomed to assume, with strange disregard of notorious facts, that nobody need find any difficulty in deciding the true meaning of any text whatever. With the permission of the House, he would give a few illustrations of the Evangelical method of dealing with the inspired book; from which it would very clearly appear, that when they boasted of appealing to the Bible, they only appealed to their own version of it, that is, to themselves; and that their favourite shibboleth, "the Bible, and the Bible only," meant simply, as Dean Blunt had well observed, "*my* interpretation of the Bible, and not yours."

Thus, when our Lord said to His priests: "I give to *you* the keys of the kingdom of heaven," it is plain, according to the Evangelicals, that He meant: "I give to *no man* the keys of the kingdom of heaven."

When He declared: "Whosesoever sins *you* remit, they are remitted;" beyond doubt He wished them to understand: "I particularly withhold from *you* the power to remit sin."

When He gave the promise to his Church: "I am with you always, even to the end of the world;" manifestly He designed to say: "I am with you only to the end of the third or fourth century, after which I shall desert you until the sixteenth."

When He announced: "I will send the Holy Ghost, and He shall guide you into *all* truth;" it is clearer than the day that He wished to tell them: "The Holy Ghost will teach you just so much of truth as each individual can gather for himself from the private study of the Scriptures."

When He made the wonderful statement: "The gates of hell shall *never* prevail against the Church;" even children can see that He meant: "Hell shall triumph over the Church for eight hundred years and more."

Finally, when he exclaimed: "He that will not hear the Church let him be to thee as the heathen and the publican;" how obvious the interpretation: "He that will not hear the Church, let him be to thee as a brother; provided only he read the Bible, and call himself an Evangelical."

As the Evangelicals dealt in this manner with the words of the Master, it was not surprising that they should treat His apostles with the same derision. A few examples would suffice:—

If St. Paul said: "A man that is a heretic *reject;*" everybody perceives that he meant: "Particularly *court* the company of heretics, and gladly join in prayer with them."

If he exhorted: "Let there be *no* divisions," what is more evident than this truth: "*Without* divisions the human mind will be enslaved by priestcraft."

If he taught that there should be "no schisms in the body," surely it was equivalent to saying: "Let the body be made up of schisms."

If he affirmed: "The works of the flesh are manifest, which are *sects*," it was precisely as if he had said: "Now, sects are the first-fruits of the Spirit."

If, alluding to holy marriage, he observed: "It is good for a man *not* to touch a woman," how manifest the meaning: "Everybody should marry, and particularly priests."

If, again, he said: "He that is married is divided," how transparent the scriptural lesson: "All men *ought* to marry, in order that they *may* be divided."

If, once more, he admonished Christians:. "He that is *not*

married careth for the Lord," how patent the Apostolic counsel: "Make haste to marry, especially the bishops and clergy, that you may *cease* to care for the Lord."

He would now proceed to give illustrations of a different kind, and from a different source. He was anxious to show, as a mere matter of fairness to Mr. Kidds, that his method and that of his party in the Church was not inconsistent with the language of the Articles, which would supply remarkable specimens of the same kind. For this reason he felt at liberty to remain in communion with men whose views of Christianity were diametrically opposed to his own. Both could plead the approval, silent or spoken, of their common mother. The maxim, "*Quieta non movere*"—which in their communion might be interpreted, "Peace at any price"—was not to be lightly esteemed; and, perhaps, in the event of any future revision of the Thirty-Nine Articles, the sense of that salutary maxim might be embodied in theological terms, so as to constitute the fortieth of their number.

The examples he proposed to add were as follows; each was unique of its kind:—There was the example dogmatic; the example critical; and the example evasive. And, first, for the example *dogmatic.*

The Twenty-eighth Article pronounced that the Catholic doctrine of the Sacrament of the Altar is "repugnant to the plain words of Scripture." Now the plain words were: "This *is* my body." Consequently, when our Lord said: "This *is* my body," the plain meaning of His words was: "This is *not* my body." By parity of reasoning, had our Lord said: "This is *not* my body," the plain meaning of his words would have been—Transubstantiation! On the same principle, when there came a voice from Heaven: "This *is* my beloved Son," it is repugnant to the plain words of Scripture to suppose that the Eternal Father revealed the Hypostatic Union. But had the Eternal Father affirmed: "This is *not* my beloved Son," the plain meaning would have been, what, in short, every good Christian erroneously believes to be true. He (Dean Primitive) had always regarded this statement of the Articles as an intentional and ingenious irony, of which the Bible theory was the object; and it was with this reservation that he swore to it at his ordination. For if the statement were seriously made, it would be perhaps the most eccentric defiance of common sense, and common honesty, with which the literature of the world had hitherto furnished them.

Next for the example *critical*.

He (Dean Primitive) had found himself some years since attending a parish meeting in the north of England, presided over by a clergyman of great repute. The question under discussion was the best mode of treating controversial subjects in their divided Church. One clergyman strongly objected to all controversy, on the ground that it quenched charity, and led to no practical result. Immediately arose another, who declared in a loud voice, and with great energy of manner, that he had the authority of "Paul himself" for the condemnation of so wretched and unscriptural an opinion. For did not Paul say, that "*without* controversy, great is the mystery of godliness," and could he more clearly imply that *with* controversy all the mystery vanishes? (Great laughter, during which Mr. Kidds rose, as if to leave the room, but appeared to change his mind.)

Thirdly, there was the example *evasive*.

At an Archidiaconal meeting in a small town in Wiltshire, the discussion at dinner turned upon fasting. It was a Friday, and he must confess that the dinner provided by the landlord of the inn, who was probably not a theologian, was both ample and succulent, including a haunch of venison, to which all had done justice. Several of the younger clergy maintained, whether from a tardy sentiment of remorse he could not say, the scriptural duty of fasting. This was indignantly denied by an incumbent of the school of Mr. Kidds. Hard pressed by various texts, and especially by the express words of St. Paul, from which there was no escape, he exclaimed, after a few moments of painful deliberation: " Paul was a young man when he enjoined fasting, and probably became more scriptural afterwards."

Before resuming his seat, he would beg to offer his humble contribution toward the solution of the question proposed by Dr. Easy. It would certainly be sin and madness to deny the existence of God, but it would, he thought, be wrong to consider it heresy—at least in an Evangelical. He very much feared that in that particular section of their Church heresy was impossible: because heresy was only the "choice" of one's own religion, and the Low-Church theory required every Protestant to make that choice deliberately for himself. Given the right which modern "liberty" conferred on every Protestant of gathering his own religion from the Bible, it would be unreasonable to call any man a sinner, and absurd to call him a heretic. A Christian, on the Low-Church theory, could only be a heretic when he differed from himself, and persisted in wilful disobedience to his own opinions. Heresy, therefore, as far as they were concerned, was a word that had lost all sense and meaning. A man might be a *criminal* in denying the existence of God, but he could not by any possibility be a heretic. The Low-Church party had conferred this boon on Christian England, that it had rendered heresy, which used to be the greatest of crimes, an absolute impossibility for anybody to commit.

But if he must speak for himself on the question proposed by Dr. Easy, he had only to reply that the Fathers and the first four General Councils believed there *was* a God, and that they were the safest guides on every point of Catholic belief.

DR. CANDOUR demanded: How should the *poor* know anything about the Fathers or the General Councils?

DEAN PRIMITIVE: Their clergy would instruct them.

DR. CANDOUR: But if their clergy differed?

DEAN PRIMITIVE: The Councils did not differ, nor the Fathers.

DR. CANDOUR: That might be true: but certainly the clergy differed quite as much about the Councils and the Fathers as they did about the Bible. So that, after all, it came to this, that the Puseyites' *private* reading of the records of the early Church was the same in principle with Mr. Kidds' *private* reading of the Bible; with this advantage to the latter, that every one can read the Bible who can read at all, but not one person in a million can read the Councils or the Fathers. Now "salvation by scholarship alone" was a theory that had its disadvantages on the score of its exclusiveness. Besides, it was a fact that many Anglicans, like Dr. Ives, an American Bishop, were converted to the Roman Church, chiefly by the study of the Fathers and the Councils. These converts argued that the ancient writers required a living interpreter equally with Holy writ; whereas the Puseyites affirmed that every man was born a Sovereign Pontiff to sit in judgment on the early Church! Deans Blunt and Primitive had been severe on Mr. Kidds, he thought unjustly, on the ground that Bible Christianity was a cloak for private fancies and conceits; but he would like to be informed—since the Roman Church, the Greek Church, and every other church, claimed to be the true and sole successors of the early Church—where was the difference between the *private* reading of the Bible and the *private* reading of antiquity?

(Dean Primitive declining to continue the discussion, Convocation broke up into various groups, and the sitting was temporarily suspended. Several reverend gentlemen produced sandwiches, or other temperate food, the consumption of which tended to allay excitement by impeding conversation. Dean Pompous alone left the Hall, as if disdaining equally the food and the discourse; but as he was observed, on returning a few minutes later, to replace a gold tooth-pick in his waistcoat pocket, it was inferred that he had chosen to take his refreshment apart. When order and silence had at length been restored, the debate was resumed, without any signs of diminished interest.)

THE PROFESSOR OF THEOLOGY, responding to a general call of the House, now manifested his intention to address the assembly.

It was no doubt true, he observed, that the appreciation of the Evangelical party, with which Dean Primitive had favoured them, was substantially exact. Their somewhat exaggerated Protestantism had been playfully rebuked; and he was free to admit that it was the product of ideas and sentiments which did not find their source in common sense nor in rational religion. But he was no less convinced, and he thought the moment had arrived to make this observation, if only as a matter of justice to the High-Church party, and to protect them from a purely invidious calumny, that, in point of essential unmitigated Protestantism, the Puseyites surpassed their

Low-Church rivals as much as they did in ability and learning. It had been observed by Dean Blunt that "self" was the *alpha* and *omega* of the Low-Church party. But if self was the Bible at Exeter Hall, it was also the supreme Pontiff at Oxford. "The Bible interpreted by the Church," meant "both interpreted by myself;" and "the Fathers interpreted by the Church," meant "*my* opinion of the Fathers interpreted by *my* opinion of the Church." Add to these the ultra-Protestant formula, "the Bible, and the Bible only," —which meant simply "my own interpretation of that book, not yours;"—and it was plain to common sense that all three formulas were absolutely one in principle. The only real difference between them would be found in their accidental developments. One illustration of this fact was as good as a thousand. Some years ago, as his reverend colleagues might remember, the late Rev. John Keble preached a remarkable sermon, of which the Rev. A. T. Russell, though a clergyman of the same communion, publicly declared that it was "inconsistent with the profession of Christianity"—meaning, of course, Mr. Russell's Christianity. In this case the private interpretation of the Bible was arrayed against the private interpretation of the Fathers; and the result of the conflict was that each advocate indulged in a perfectly harmless damnation of the other, both remaining authorised ministers of the same wisely liberal and tolerant Church.

The truth was, that Puseyism—to use once more a convenient term which usage had consecrated—was simply ultra-Protestantism, *plus* twice its pretensions, and *minus* half its cant. Self, he repeated, was the sole pontiff on both sides, but self assumed far more gigantic dimensions in the High than in the Low-Church school. To sit in judgment on the Fathers and the Councils *as well as* on the Bible; to instruct the doctors where they were right, and admonish the saints where they were wrong; to tell the Church what it was her duty to teach, and obey her only so long as she consented to obey themselves;—this was evidently a more courageous self-worship than to be content with the humbler privilege of manipulating texts. For this reason, he had always said, and would now repeat, that, in point of essential and uncompromising Protestantism, High-Churchmen had no rivals, whether in the Church of England or in any other community. They alone, who were sometimes charged with unfaithfulness to the Reformation, used *all* the licence which it gave. To assert the principle of authority, whilst daily repudiating it in practice; to claim to be "Catholic," while cheerfully remaining out of communion with any church, school, or party in the whole Christian world; this was the special glory of gentlemen who had always far surpassed the modest and timid warfare of their neighbours, and contrived to enjoy the luxury of protesting at the same moment against the Roman Church, their own church, and every other church. It was true, indeed, that in order not to be quite alone in the world, they affected to transfer their homage to a purely imaginary *primitive* Church, which existed only in their own brain, and their pretended obedience to which relieved them from the irksome duty of yielding the slightest obedience to any other. This submission to a Church, which had ceased to exist for many centuries, if it had ever existed at all, was, in his opinion, the most ingenious of all Protestant contrivances for submitting to nothing and nobody.

(Dean Primitive and Archdeacon Chasuble here rose together in much excitement, but the latter being called upon by the House, said): He apologised for interrupting the learned Professor, but his feelings overpowered him, and he could not remain silent. He had always regarded Anglicanism, for he declined to repeat the opprobrious nickname employed by the Professor, as the only combination hitherto attempted of authority with private judgment.

THE PROFESSOR: That might have been, and probably was, the original programme of the party, but private judgment had soon strangled authority, as might have been safely predicted, and no sect of Christians of that or any other age were so contemptuous of all authority, whether enthroned at Lambeth or in the Vatican, as those who were commonly called Puseyites. A Papist said, and was at least consistent with his profession; "My church is my teacher; therefore I obey her." A Puseyite said, not in word, but in act; "My church is my pupil, therefore I instruct her." The difference was admirably stated by a Frenchman, when he ingeniously observed: "The Puseyite says, 'L'Eglise, c'est *moi*;' the Catholic says, 'L'Eglise, c'est *nous*.'"

There was not, he conceived, in the annals of human religions—of which the number was now almost beyond arithmetical calculation

—so singular a paradox as that which was displayed in **Puseyite** theology. The claims of a Leo the Great, or a Gregory the Seventh, which at least, whatever Protestants might think of them, were cordially admitted both in their own generation and in those which followed it, were only the utterances of timid self-abasement, compared with the super-œcumenical dogmatism of their High-Church friends. " Obey me," said these gentlemen to their disciples, "for obedience is the prerogative of the laity; but I obey nobody except my own interpretation of the Fathers, or of such of them as I approve, because my church is not yet sufficiently Catholic to deserve my obedience. At present I am obliged to create a church for you, because nothing worthy of the name is found just now on earth. The day will come when she will have been sufficiently taught by me, will cease to be Protestant without becoming Roman, and then I shall be able to obey the Church, because, having learned from me the exact form of primitive Christianity, which exists nowhere at present but in my own ideal conception, the Church will have come again into corporate existence, and will be worthy of your dutiful regard. It will then no longer be necessary for me, as it is unfortunately at present, to cumulate in my own person the functions of the Pope, the Saints, the Fathers, the General Councils, and Almighty God."

(Considerable agitation followed this speech, during which the sitting was suspended for some minutes.)

The REV. LAVENDER KIDDS observed, as soon as the composure of the Assembly was restored, that, however forcible the remarks of the learned Professor might be as applied to Puseyism, he had shown that he was unwilling to grapple with the grand principle of Bible Christianity, of which he was the humble advocate.

THE PROFESSOR intended no disrespect to Mr. Kidds and his party. Bible Christianity, since he must speak of it, (though he thought that former speakers had sufficiently disposed of the subject,) was only less preposterous than the rival theory which he had just ventured to describe. It required personal infallibility in all who professed it. It simply transferred to the individual the supernatural prerogative which the Romanist attributed to his Church. It was obvious to common sense that if Mr. Kidds could interpret a particular translation of the Scriptures, so as to know infallibly both how much was necessary to salvation, and exactly what was necessary to be believed about it, he must himself be personally infallible.

MR. KIDDS would confidently insist that the cases were not identical, because the interpretation of the Bible did not require the monstrous faculty assumed by that apostate Church, the Holy Book being *plain* on all points which were "necessary to salvation."

THE PROFESSOR, being anxious to satisfy Mr. Kidds, would reply that the plainness of the Bible was not a point to be discussed until it could first be proved that the Bible was their sole authority in matters of faith. But was this assumption consistent with historical facts? Before the invention of printing in the fifteenth century, not one man in a million could possess a copy of the Scriptures. He might add that not one man in ten thousand could have read the Bible, even if he had possessed it. Printing, therefore, on Mr. Kidds' theory, was that Second Dispensation, which was intended by Almighty God to supplant the authority of a Living Church. And, moreover, whatever Mr. Kidds' private views on printing, at least he must confess that, but for the assiduous care with which, through more than a thousand years, the Roman Church preserved and multiplied the manuscripts of Holy Writ, neither he nor any other Protestant could have known that there had ever been a Bible at all.

MR. KIDDS exclaimed with energy: The Roman Church forbids the Bible to the people!

THE PROFESSOR: The Roman Church does just the contrary. She *compels* the people to hear the Gospels and Epistles read from the pulpit every Sunday morning; reading, moreover, the same Epistles and Gospels—selected with a wisdom which seemed more than human, and revealed a truly marvellous comprehension of their divine meaning—which the Church of England had appropriated from her Missal. What the Church of Rome does *not* permit is, that every one should interpret for himself the most difficult book that ever was written; that every ignorant fanatic or conceited curate should mount a pulpit and expound a private gospel of his own; and if the Roman Church required justification in that prudent course, she had only to point to the chaos of ideas engendered by English Protestantism to prove that of all the wild delusions that had ever possessed the human mind, the Printing theory was the most absurd.

MR. KIDDS was not to be shaken from his first position: that upon all the points which are necessary to salvation the Bible is *plain*.

THE PROFESSOR, turning to Mr. Kidds with a smile, replied: Every doctrine was plain to those who chose to believe it, and clothed in densest obscurity to those who did not. Baptism, the Apostolic Succession, Sacramental Confession, the Real Presence, were plainly necessary to salvation to all who liked them, and as plainly unnecessary to all who disliked them. The Bible plain! Why, the awful doctrines of the Holy Trinity, the Divinity of Christ, and the Atonement, had *all* been vehemently denied on the authority of the Bible! Was Mr. Kidds ignorant that Roman Catholics confidently quoted the Bible, from Genesis to Revelations, against Protestant doctrines? Did he know that Cardinal Bellarmine quoted more than fifty texts in proof of Purgatory, and that others quoted more than a hundred in defence of their confidence in the Blessed Virgin? (Mr. Kidds groaned aloud.) Was anything more plain to the Papist than the declaration to Peter: "Upon *this* rock I will build my church?" Was anything less ambiguous to him than the words: "This *is* my body?" Anything more decisive than the announcement: "It is a wholesome and holy thought to pray for the dead?" [ARCHDEACON JOLLY here observed to a neighbour, that the Church of England, as a quiet way of getting rid of this "unscriptural" text, ordered it to be left out, when it occurred in the Lesson for the day!] All Scripture doctrines, he repeated, were plain to those who liked them, and forced or perverted to those who did not. What was "pure gospel" to Mr. Brown was "deadly error" to Mr. Green, and the "fundamental verities" of Mr. Thompson were the "satanical delusions" of Mr.

Johnson. One half the clergy of the Church of England believed that the religion of the other half was odious in the sight of God, and yet they all read the Bible! The Bible plain! Why there was less dispute among men as to the interpretation of the Vedas, of Chinese chronology, or of Egyptian archæology, than of this plain and intelligible book, which, to the eternal dishonor of Protestant commentators, had now almost ceased to have any definite meaning whatever, because every imaginable meaning had been defended by some, and denied by others. Plain! when such a man as St. Augustine—who was a professor of rhetoric before he became a Christian, and a man of gigantic intellect—frankly avowed that "the Bible contained more things which he could *not*, than which he could understand." Plain! when the two most cherished dogmas of Protestantism—the observance of the Sunday, and the reading of the New Testament—are nowhere commanded by our Lord, the Evangelists, or the Apostles. Plain! when Bishop Colenso, in writing to the *Times*, could quote *eleven* texts of Scripture to prove that prayer ought not to be offered to our Blessed Lord. Plain! when their own Church flatly denied it, and admitted that she could not infallibly *know* the truth, by honestly confessing that she could not infallibly *teach* it. Plain! when every bishop and every clergyman, in every charge and every sermon, proved that it was not. Every shuffling decision of the Privy Council proved that it was not. Every gossiping conclave at Exeter Hall proved that it was not. Every conflicting debate of Convocation proved that it was not. The very heathen proved that it was not; for they jeeringly replied to Protestant missionaries, "Since you all read the Book, why don't you all agree about it?" Finally, a hundred sects outside the Church, and five hundred within her, proved that it was not, and that its boasted plainness came at last to this, that the only common truth which all men agreed to derive from it was the historical doctrine of an historical Saviour.

MR. KIDDS would add, with devout gratitude, "and the cordial abhorrence of Popery."

THE PROFESSOR would ask permission to waive, at least for the moment, that profoundly philosophical dogma, observing only that at least Roman Catholics did not gather that doctrine from the Bible, and that they were the largest body of Christians in the world. Meanwhile, he would request Mr. Kidds to observe that Bible Christianity had this inconvenience, that it degraded all Truth to Opinion; and whilst it ridiculed infallibility as diffused throughout the Roman Church, it made itself far more ridiculous by claiming for every individual what it denied to the largest and most ancient of communions. The truth was, that Protestantism, on the Bible-theory, was, in principle, "Popery," multiplied by as many individuals as there were Protestants in the world. Instead of one infallible Pope,—who at least was never known to reverse the dogmatical decisions of those who had gone before him,—they had now got several millions of infallible individuals, who were incessantly occupied in contradicting one another. He did not know that they had gained much by the change. If the aggregate infallibility of the Roman Church was hard to stomach, the personal infallibility of every one of your neighbours was simply intolerable. But what he desired most to recommend to the notice of Mr. Kidds and his party was this, that none went so far as they to discredit infallibility, by the manner in which they claimed it for themselves; and none went so far to prove it, by the manner in which they denied it to the Catholic Church. To quote the words of a modern Roman Catholic: "Protestants, by denying the Catholic theory, have proved the impossibility of knowing what is necessary to salvation; and by asserting the Protestant theory, they have presented to the world the prodigious spectacle of every man differing at every point of his own (hypothetical) infallibility."

DEAN PRIMITIVE would venture to ask the Professor, who seemed to display equal contempt for both parties in his own Church, while he manifested at least an intellectual sympathy with Roman claims, how he could reconcile it to his conscience to retain his Professorial Chair?

THE PROFESSOR replied: It made one smile to be asked in those days, whether any particular opinion, or set of opinions, involved disloyalty to the Established Church. What opinion was *not* held within its communion? Were not Dr. Wilberforce and Dr. Colenso, Dr. Hamilton and Dr. Baring, equally bishops of the

Church of England? Were not Dr. Pusey and Mr. Jowett at the same moment her Professors; Brother Ignatius and Mr. Bellew her ministers; Archdeacon Denison and Dr. M'Neile her distinguished ornaments and preachers? Yet their religions differed almost as widely as Buddhism from Calvinism, or the philosophy of Aristotle from that of Mr. Martin Tupper. A good many things were dead amongst them besides the Test Act. He doubted if even Hoadley would be prosecuted now, and was quite sure he would not be prosecuted with success. Dr. Hampden had been called in an Anglican paper "as well-known a heretic as Arius was," and yet was as truly an Anglican bishop as Ken or Jeremy Taylor. The "Essays and Reviews" were condemned only the other day by a majority of Convocation; yet one of their ablest contributors continued to be chaplain to the Queen, who was the head of their Church. Dr. Stanley had been excommunicated by Dr. Wordsworth, yet this only confirmed his appointment as Dean of Westminster, and might even materially assist him in becoming Archbishop of Canterbury. Resign his office for conscience sake! continued the Professor: he was really incapable of an act at once so presumptuous and so unnecessary. Who was he that he should teach a communion so reluctant to enforce them the forgotten claims of conscience? He would advise his friend Dean Primitive to be very cautious in recommending "resignation" to those from whom he differed. If an Anglican minister must resign because his opinions were at variance with those of some other Anglican minister, every soul among them would have to retire—from the Archbishop of Canterbury down to the last licentiate from Durham or St. Bees. (Great laughter.) Resignation would be a clumsy remedy for the evils which they all confessed; it would cure the disease, but it would kill the patient. Other members of his party were more worldly-wise than Dean Primitive. Mr. Bennett had lately addressed a letter to Dr. Pusey, in which, while declaring that their controversy with the Low-Church clergy was a matter of "life and death," he argued that the latter ought to be allowed to "remain in their communion." If he approved th's plea,—as consistent with the spirit and the history of the Anglican Church, whose motto was, "Live and let live," and which had always been more solicitous to keep men of different religions within her pale than to force them to go out,—he would not conceal that, from another point of view, the language of Mr. Bennett filled him with disgust and contempt. It was a fresh proof how little men of his school really cared for the mysterious doctrines about which they talked so glibly, since they were quite willing to "remain in communion" with men who flatly denied them, and even publicly insisted that the latter had as good a right as themselves to be teachers in the Anglican Church! What could such men care about what they impudently called "*the Truth?*" (Sensation.)

But he would ask Dean Primitive, who was probably more sincere than others of his party, why any man should "resign," whatever his opinions might be, when the Privy Council had decided that it was lawful to hold *either* of two opposite doctrines? If there was only *one* dogma in the Church of England, why did she tolerate within her pale *two* discordant dogmas upon almost every fact and tenet of Christianity? Why did she treat every article of the faith as the false mother was willing to treat the child not her own, and consent to *kill* by cutting it in two? Why did Privy Council permit no definite doctrine; and Convocation agree upon none? Why was Archdeacon Denison tried for preaching the Real Presence, and let off because it was proved that he did so; while Dr. Forbes was convicted of holding Transubstantiation, and excused because he engaged *not to teach it?* Why did Dr. Sumner appoint Mr. Gorham to a benefice because he denied Regeneration in Baptism, and the Sovereign make Dr. Philpotts a bishop because he believed it? Why did the Bishop of Salisbury deliver a charge in which he informed his diocese that more than half the English clergy were heretics, while the Bishop of Durham deposed a Rural Dean for teaching the very doctrines which the Bishop of Salisbury declared to be divine? Why did the Queen make Dr. Colenso her bishop at Natal, though her own Courts declared that she had no power to do so, yet suffer her Bishop at Cape Town to try to remove him by an authority as visionary as her own? Why did Dr. Pusey advocate the union of the English Church with those of Rome and Moscow, excluding the Scandinavian and other Protestant bodies; while Dr. Tait, rejoicing in the ministry of Mr. Spurgeon, proposed to exclude both Rome and Moscow, and to unite the Anglican See of London with the Tabernacle of a Baptist preacher? But it was idle to ask the "why" of all the monstrous phenomena which were constantly passing before their eyes, and which were now too much a matter of course to excite even the passing curiosity of the public. They proved—and this was his answer to Dean Primitive—that the only real disqualification for remaining in the Church of England was, not the holding opinions contradicted by those around you, but the holding any definite opinion whatever. That alone, he was prepared to maintain, was the sole unpardonable inconsistency with the principles of the Anglican Church.

DR. THEORY hoped that the Professor would not resume his seat, without favoring the House with his opinion on Dr. Easy's hypothesis.

THE PROFESSOR must decline to give his own opinion, though of course he had one, on the question proposed by Dr. Easy; but he had no objection to state how he conceived it ought to be answered by the so-called Bible-Christian. That answer might be as follows:

The existence of a Church assumes the existence of a God; therefore, the denial of a God would be the same with a denial of a Church. But the Church of England is a fact. Her teaching may be doubtful or contradictory, but her existence as a politico-ecclesiastical institution, professing belief in a God, is beyond dispute. It would, therefore, be heresy in the Bible-Christian to deny the existence of *a* God, but it was quite open to him to believe in any *kind* of divinity he might prefer, and to clothe Him with whatever attributes the Privy Council had permitted Him to retain. For example: the Justice of God was evidently an open question, because the Privy Council had decided that punishment was not necessarily eternal. The Truthfulness of God was very doubtful, because the Privy Council had decreed that God's revelation to man was, perhaps, not plenarily inspired. The Faithfulness of God was more than obscure, because the Privy Council had ruled that Baptism was not necessarily the Sacrament of Regeneration. Finally, the Unity of God was impossible, because the Privy Council had repeatedly affirmed that truth was not one but manifold. The Bible-Christian might, therefore, argue that it would be heresy to deny the existence of *a* God, because, as he had said, the existence of the Church implied the existence of some kind of divinity; but that it would *not* be heresy to deny any one of His attributes, because, if the supreme Anglican tribunal spoke truly, it was hardly possible that God should have any.

DR. EASY was grateful to the learned Professor for the light which he had thrown upon the question which he had ventured to submit to their examination. The debate had elicited precisely the conclusion at which he desired to arrive. It was, however, to be regretted that the Privy Council, whose chief aim was to decide nothing, had really decided, by implication, that the existence of God was an open question. Such a decision might be fruitful of evil. Every one was privately aware that, in the Church of England, nothing was necessarily anything. Still, it was a pity to burden the consciences of good men by *obliging* them to think that they must necessarily take the unnecessary view of Christianity. It had really come to this, thanks to the bungling caution of the Privy Council, that the only dogma now left to them, besides the fallibility of their Church, might be thus expressed: "The necessity of taking the non-necessary view of everything;" or perhaps, as a substitute for Creed, Catechism, and Articles, they might enunciate the whole scope of Anglican theology in this one proposition: "Unbelief, considered as generally necessary to salvation."

On the other hand, he would be the last to deny their obligations to the Privy Council, which was the mildest and best-bred of human tribunals. What could surpass the considerateness with which it said to every defendant summoned to its bar: "Pray, do not let me hamper your Christian freedom, nor interfere with your disbelieving half or the whole of Christianity. You object to Baptism? Well, well, the Church will not be severe upon you for that. You doubt Plenary Inspiration? Then pray, my dear sir, don't believe it. You detest the notion of a Sacrifice? We have already decided that there is no such thing as an altar in the Church of England. You are shocked at the idea of the eternity of punishment? We will meet your views, and invent a new kind of Anglican Purgatory for you instead." Considering that every possible variety of belief and unbelief existed in their Church, and had existed from the beginning, was it a light advantage to possess an authority so mild and gentle, whose decisions were so admirably adapted to the circumstances of the times? "Come to me," it seemed to say, "whenever you feel the burden of any doctrine or tenet, and I will do my best to arrange it comfortably for you. Place the fullest confidence in me. I know the history and the character of the Church whose voice I am; and, as I have never yet obliged you to believe anything to which you object, you may repose in the tranquil assurance that I never will."

ARCHDEACON JOLLY was so much impressed by the observations of the preceding speaker, that he thought they should not separate without expressing, in a more formal way, their gratitude to the Privy Council. He was inclined to propose something more practical than a barren vote of thanks. Let the now unmeaning words of their Prayer-Book be altered so as to be in harmony with facts and with the new decisions. It would be something to make a beginning, which their critics scoffingly affirmed Convocation was quite unable to do. He would move the following vote: "That that portion of the Catechism be recast which teaches that there are 'two sacraments, as generally necessary to salvation;' and that, in answer to the question, 'How many sacraments are there?' the clause should stand thus: 'Two only, as *formerly* necessary to salvation, but one of them not so necessary now as it used to be.'"

DEAN BLUNT feared the new formula would hardly satisfy the requirements of the age. He thought that if they took the sense of the country, it would be more truthful to render the clause thus: "Two only, as equally *unnecessary* to salvation, but baptism to be viewed as rather an impediment to salvation than otherwise."

ARCHDEACON JOLLY would consider the amendment during the recess.

THE REV. LAVENDER KIDDS here rose in much excitement. He would boldly declare his opinion that the debate of that day was a disgrace to a Protestant House of Convocation. He trusted that Convocation would deem it a solemn duty not to separate without, at least, renewing its protest against the iniquitous Church of Rome. He would presume to add that, by that step alone, it could repair much that was unscriptural and unsound in the discussion of that day. He was prepared, if necessary, to make a formal motion to the effect that "Convocation continues to regard with horror the corruption and superstitions of Popery." This was the first and holiest duty of every vital Christian.

ARCHDEACON JOLLY doubted whether the universal *Nego* of Mr. Kidds and his friends could combat successfully the eternal *Credo* of two hundred millions of Catholics. However, he was quite willing to consider Mr. Kidds' proposition; but he must be excused if he did so from his own point of view.

There was a large class of persons in this country, continued the Archdeacon, who, having no definite religion of their own, and being slenderly endowed with common sense, were indebted to the Roman Catholic Church both for employment and maintenance. Let Mr. Kidds restrain his excitement; he would explain his meaning. He did not, of course, include Mr. Kidds among the class in question, though he believed that gentleman would willingly accept the statement of Sterne, who candidly confessed, that "when he had little to say, or little to give his people, he had recourse to the abuse of Popery. Hence he called it his 'Cheshire Cheese.' It had a twofold advantage; it cost him very little, and he found by experience that nothing satisfied so well the hungry appetite of his congregation. They always devoured it greedily."

Perhaps Mr. Kidds was not aware that in his zeal to hasten the downfall of Popery,—which, even according to modern prophets, had still a few years to last, and which, judging by a recent tour he had made on the Continent, presented anything but a moribund aspect,—he was in violent opposition with many active and devoted Protestants. The persons to whom he alluded were, at this moment, full of anxiety, lest Popery should perish too soon! They could not afford to say farewell to their old friend at present, and desired only to keep him on his legs a little longer. Mr. Kidds was probably ignorant that a society had recently been formed in London, in connection, he believed, with the Protestant Reformation Society, to which it was designed to act as a timely and important auxiliary. The title of this new association was: "*Society for considering the best means of keeping alive the corruptions of Popery in the interests of Gospel truth.*" It was, of course, a strictly secret organization, but he had been favoured, he knew not why, with a copy of the prospectus, and as he had no intention of becoming a member, he would communicate it to the House. It appeared from this document, and could be confirmed from other sources, that a deputation was sent last year to Rome, to obtain a private interview with the Pope, in order to entreat His Holiness *not* to reform a single Popish corruption. He was assured that they had reason to believe, he did not know on what grounds, that the Pope was about to introduce extensive reforms, beginning with the substitution of the Thirty-Nine Articles for the creed of Pope Pius, and a permanent Anglican Convocation in lieu of an occasional œcumenical Council. A handsome present was entrusted to the deputation, and a liberal contribution to the Peter's Pence Fund. The motives set forth in the preamble of the address presented to His Holiness were, in substance, of the following nature:—They urged that a very large body of most respectable clergymen, who had no personal ill-will towards the present occupant of the Holy See, had maintained themselves and their families in comfort for many years exclusively by the abuse of Popery; and if Popery were taken away, they could not but contemplate the probable results with uneasiness and alarm. Moreover, many eminent members of the profession had gained a reputation for Evangelical wit, learning, and piety, as well as high dignities in the Church of England, by setting forth in their sermons and at public meetings, with all their harrowing details, the astounding abominations of the Church of Rome. The petitioners implored His Holiness not to be indifferent to the position of these gentlemen. Many of their number had privately requested the deputation to plead their cause with the amiable and benevolent Pius IX. Thus the great and good Dr. M'Nickel represented respectfully that he had filled his church, and let all his pews, during three-and-twenty years, by elegantly slandering priests and nuns, and powerfully illustrating Romish superstitions. A clergyman of noble birth had attained to the honors of the episcopate by handling alternately the same subjects, and a particularly pleasing doctrine of the Millennium, and had thus been enabled to confer a valuable living on his daughter's husband, who otherwise could not have hoped to obtain one. An eminent canon of an old Roman Catholic abbey owed his distinguished position, which he hoped to be allowed to retain, to the fact of his having proved so clearly that the Pope was Antichrist; and earnestly entreated His Holiness to do nothing to forfeit that character. A well-known doctor of Anglican divinity was on the point of quitting the country in despair of gaining a livelihood, when the idea of preaching against Popery was suggested to him, and he had now reason to rejoice that he had abandoned the foolish scheme of emigration. Even a High-Church bishop had been so hampered by suspicions of Romanistic tendencies, which were perfectly unfounded, that he had only saved himself from general discredit by incessant abuse of Popery, though he was able to say, in self-defence, that he did not believe a word of his own invectives. Finally, a young clergyman, who had not hitherto much distinguished himself, having often but vainly solicited a member of his congregation to favor his evangelical attachment, at length hit upon a new expedient, and preached so ravishing a discourse on the matrimonial prohibitions of the Romish Church, and drew so appalling a picture of the domestic infelicities of the Romish priesthood, that on the following Monday morning the young lady made him an offer of her hand and fortune. It was hoped that His Holiness would give due consideration to interests so grave and manifold, and not peril them by hasty reforms, which nobody desired, and which nobody would receive with satisfaction.

Another class of clergymen appealed still more urgently to the forbearance of the Pope. They represented that they were in the habit of realising large sums by the publication of prophetical works, of which the whole interest turned upon the approximate destruction of "the Beast," and that, while they indicated, by the help of the Apocalypse, the precise hour of his fall, they yet managed to put off the final catastrophe from year to year, and could hardly supply the successive editions which the curiosity of the public demanded. They hoped that His Holiness would do nothing rash and imprudent which might compromise their particular industry. One of these gentlemen ingenuously confessed that without Antichrist, who was his best friend, and the invaluable book of Revelations, which was his chief source of income, he saw nothing before him but the workhouse. He begged to forward to the Pope a copy of each of his works, including the following:—
"Horns of the Beast," neatly bound, with gilt edges; "Antichrist,"

handsomely got up, "positively his last appearance in 1864, in consequence of other engagements," with new editions in 1865, 1866, and 1867; also, "Answer to an insolent pamphlet, entitled 'The *Number and Street* of the Beast proved to be that of the Rev. Dr. Comeagain.'"

Lastly, even members of Parliament to whom nature had not been prodigal in intellectual endowments, urged with great force that they were able to get on their legs, and to stay there, detailing the prodigious incidents of conventual turpitude; making the blood to curdle, and the hair to stand on end, by thrilling narratives of nuns immured, and clanking chains, and bereaved mothers, invoking in agonised chorus, "Liberty and Mr. Newdegate." They hoped the Pope would see in this fact the necessity of caution, lest he should unwittingly put to silence more than one independent member of Parliament, deprive an illustrious assembly of its chief amusement, and rashly change the composition of the British House of Commons.

DEAN POMPOUS inquired (with a somewhat thick utterance but with great dignity of manner) whether he understood the Archdeacon to say that he had actually seen this document?

ARCHDEACON JOLLY: He had certainly said so; it had been shown to him in Rome by Cardinal Antonelli.

DEAN POMPOUS might perhaps hazard a suspicion as to its authenticity?

ARCHDEACON JOLLY: Had such a document been found in London or Edinburgh, the suspicion might be reasonable, but, having been seen in Rome, the evidence for its authenticity must be accepted in the inverse ratio of its credibility. This principle would be easily admitted by Protestants of the school of Mr. Kidds. They had only to turn for proof to the treatise on Moral Evidence lately put forth by the "*Anglo-Metropolitan and General Superstition Repelling Association.*" At page 127 of that work they would find the following postulate:

> "Let it be granted that, in all which relates to Rome, the Babylon of the Apocalypse, a thing is more or

less true in proportion to its improbability; and that those things alone are absolutely certain of which it can be demonstrated that they never could by any possibility have happened."

(At this point, as nobody rose to continue the discussion, it seemed likely to close abruptly. Several reverend divines took their hats, and appeared about to retire, when it was whispered that Archdeacon Chasuble had intimated his desire to address the House on the twofold question of Authority in the English, and Infallibility in the Catholic Church. Lively attention appeared to be excited by this announcement, and the retiring members eagerly resumed their seats.)

ARCHDEACON CHASUBLE would begin by assuring his colleagues that they would be disappointed if they thought he was going to claim infallibility for the Church of England. (Some laughter, which was immediately suppressed by loud cries of "Order.") He had deep convictions, but he trusted that he was neither a dreamer nor an enthusiast. He would not claim for his Church a gift which she had always repudiated. He began therefore by admitting that infallibility could not reside in a Church which, in the first hour of her existence, had proclaimed to the world that the whole of Christendom, including all the Apostolic Churches, had fallen into error. The original message of the Church of England to all Christian nations was in substance as follows: "The fact that I am required in the sixteenth century to teach the Catholic Church proves that the Catholic Church has become incompetent to teach. But, in recording this universal defection, I am obliged to admit that I also am liable to error. I cannot deny what is clearly involved in the fundamental axiom with which I commence my career."

But though the Anglican Church was thus confessedly fallible or human, did it follow that she was no true Church, and that her members were all out of the pale of Catholicity? God forbid. No one maintained that the Church of England was *the* Catholic Church. Her most attached members freely admitted that she was but one of several branches of that Church. Now, it was of the *Catholic* Church, of which he claimed to be a member, and not of the Church of England, that he ventured to assert, She *cannot* err. He would ask permission to prove that proposition.

If the Catholic Church were not infallible at one period of her existence,—for example, when she decreed the Canon of Holy Scripture,—what assurance had they, or could they have, that they possessed the true Bible? Saints had differed widely about it, so widely as to reject books now admitted to be canonical, while they admitted others now rejected as spurious. In the fourth century it was still an open question, till, at length, it was finally decided by the authority of the Church. If the Church were not infallible, what was the decision worth?

Again. If the Catholic Church were not infallible while she was building up her creeds and constructing her liturgies, both were a mere bundle of human opinions, which might be partly true and partly false, but could never be imposed on the conscience of mankind. What had been framed by one human authority might evidently be modified by another. It was therefore conceivable, on the hypothesis of the fallibility of the Church, that Christians had *always* had a false Bible, false creeds, and false liturgies. Nay, it was not only conceivable, but eminently probable; for how could the human beget the divine, or the certain be born of the fallible?

He had not completed his argument, but would pause to anticipate an objection. He might be fairly asked, "if the Church were infallible when she defined the Canon of Scripture, by what special act, or at what particular period, did she lose this gift of infallibility?" He replied without hesitation, *she had never lost it.* The gift was suspended for a time, by reason of the loss of unity with which it was indissolubly associated, but it might be recovered at any moment. Let the Russian, the Roman, the Greek, the Anglican, and the Oriental branches once more unite, and on the morrow of their reconciliation the dormant gift of infallibility would again revive.

THE PROFESSOR OF THEOLOGY would venture to ask the Archdeacon how half-a-dozen hostile churches, without infallibility to guide them, could possibly arrive at a common conception of the doctrines on which they had differed for ages? If the Church had not escaped falling into error, according to the Anglican hypothesis, while she still, according to the Archdeacon, possessed both unity and infallibility, how could she ever recover her position now that, as he confessed, she possessed neither the one nor the other?

ARCHDEACON CHASUBLE admitted, with deep sorrow, the force of the objection. If infallibility waited on the re-union of the warring churches,—well, it was a sad truth that there was no early prospect of its recovery. He confessed that he did not see his way to answer the objection. Still, whatever the difficulty might be, he would not the less earnestly protest against the monstrous notion, that the Catholic Church could ever abdicate the functions which she derived from her Founder, or lose the power to "teach all nations," the very object for which He expressly created her. It was an intolerable assumption that the Catholic Church, when she infallibly defined the Canon of Scripture, decreed that from that moment she was herself no longer infallible, or that she transferred the infallibility by which she decreed the Canon to the Canon whose infallibility she decreed.

No doubt they were surrounded by difficulties, and he had too much respect for truth and honesty to deny their existence. If, therefore, he were asked, why a Church which could teach with divine authority in the third or fourth centuries could no longer do so in the tenth or fourteenth, he admitted that he did not know what answer to give; because if the schisms and heresies which existed even in the apostolic age did not impair her prerogative of infallibility *then*, it was reasonable to argue that they could not produce such a consequence *now*. Evidently the Church did not become human and fallible simply because her enemies were called Luther or Cranmer instead of Cerinthus or Marcion, or because the names of Calvin or Burnet were substituted for those of Eutyches or Nestorius. If the earlier heretics could not rob the Church of the gift which God had imparted to her, certainly it was hard to see why later adversaries should be able to do so. If the Councils of Nice or Ephesus, as even the Reformers allowed, were the voice of the Holy Ghost, it was not clear why those of Florence or Trent had less claim to their obedience. But it was their sorrowful lot as Anglicans to be born to difficulties. This was their portion. Alas! they could but dimly perceive the principles of truth; their effectual application was to them impossible.

Still there were certain verities which even they could firmly grasp, and it was their duty to proclaim them aloud, whatever fatal contradictions they might seem to involve. He would declare, therefore, his own conviction that the doctrine of the fallibility of the Catholic Church was simply blasphemy, because it made God unfaithful to his promises; and palpable nonsense, because it implied that he had founded a Teaching Church without giving it the power to teach! When the Anglican homily gravely asserted that the whole Church of God,—the home of the saints and martyrs—had been "sunk in the pit of damnable idolatry by the space of nine hundred years and odd," it made the heart sick to think that they were themselves the heirs of the very men who had uttered such stupid profanity. But the founders of Anglicanism had to account for and excuse their own position in the world, and this was their way of doing it. They declared, without hesitation, that God had abandoned his own Church to what had been truly called a *Diabolical Millenium*. It almost seemed as if they were willing to pass for madmen, provided only they might be allowed to say of the Church which they had just quitted, that she was as mad as themselves.

DEAN CRITICAL had listened, thus far, with deep attention to his venerable friend, and would continue to do so to the end of his discourse; but would he permit him to interrupt him for a moment, in order to ask a question which was neither captious nor insidious? The Archdeacon evidently did not believe that the Catholic Church was infallible *now*, whatever she might have been formerly, or of course he would instantly submit to her authority; yet he distinctly affirmed that, by the first law of her nature, she *must* be so! Might they then claim him, in spite of his transcendental theories, as an advocate, after all, of the simple Protestant doctrine, that there was really no such thing as a *Teaching* Church in the world? He should be glad to think so. Would he also tell them, since the real subject of the discussion in which they were engaged was the presence or absence of *authority* in the English Church, whether he frankly admitted that that Church, having no infallibility, and therefore no divine authority, could teach no certain truth, exact no religious obedience, and anathematize no doctrinal error?

ARCHDEACON CHASUBLE was far from professing to be able to answer all the questions which might be addressed to him.

He would content himself with saying, that if there were no other ecclesiastical authority in the world than such as resided in the Church of England, it was too evident that men could possess no certainty in their religious convictions,—that they could obey no authority but what they chose for themselves,—and that heresy could not be condemned, not only because there was no authority to condemn it, but because in such a state of the Christian world it could not even exist. But to say that there could be no such thing as heresy, was evidently the same thing with saying that there could be no such thing as truth, of which heresy was simply the denial. Yet heresy was not only a crime, as they learned from St. Paul, but the greatest of all crimes, and might be called the high treason of Christians. Every other sin which man could commit was only against the laws of God, but this was against His Person and Essence. God is truth, and heresy is the worship of a lie, which is God's greatest contrary. Satan, they were told by our Lord, was "the father of lies." Heretics were therefore the dear children of Satan, who fed them with lies.

For this reason, it would seem,—because heresy was nothing but a part of Satan's warfare against God, and the greatest sin which men or devils could commit,—the Bible spoke of it only in tones of appalling menace and anathema. The Son of God had words of compassion for the adulteress, and the stern St. Paul commanded that the man guilty of incest should be admitted to pardon. Not so with heresy. There was apparently no mercy for that. St. Paul had forbidden a Christian so much as to "eat with" a heretic. And yet, at least in one of its aspects, heresy was nothing else than disobedience to the divine authority of the Church! Perhaps it was on this account that St. Augustine had intimated his opinion that wilful disobedience to the Church might probably be the sin against the Holy Ghost.

What, then, must they think of a Church in which heresy had always been impossible? Every argument in the discussion of that day had combined to prove that the Church of England not only permitted her members to be heretics, but actually made it their duty and privilege to be so. The obligation of "choosing" their religion for themselves, that is, of being heretics,—and whether they happened to choose Roman or Lutheran tenets made no kind of difference in the sin, so long as they chose for themselves,—was notoriously one of the least ambiguous injunctions of the Thirty-Nine Articles! The Church of England did not warn her members against heresy, because she did not admit its existence, and because she was conscious that she had no power to tell them with certainty what was truth.

DEAN BLUNT was unwilling to interrupt the speaker, but he felt constrained to observe that the Archdeacon seemed to revel in pointing out difficulties, of which he admitted the solution to be impossible, and which were enough to drive every member of his communion into frantic unbelief. Would he tell them plainly, Was there any living authority, old or young, in this nineteenth century, in any part of the world, which was charged by God to teach His creatures—*what is truth?*

ARCHDEACON CHASUBLE shook his head, but made no reply.

DEAN BLUNT continued: It had come then to this, that the only teacher the High-Church party would permit them, was one which had been dead and buried for about fourteen hundred years. Happy Christians! whose only chance of learning the truth, unless they took it from an authority which confessed it could not teach it, was to sift the Fathers, analyse the ecclesiastical historians, and laboriously collate the records of antiquity, written in languages which few could comprehend, all referring to a higher witness external to themselves, and equally claimed by Roman, Greek, and Anglican theologians, in confirmation of their discordant religious tenets! Certainly the Archdeacon had not afforded them much assistance in their search after Anglican "Authority." Perhaps, however, he would at least be good enough to inform them, since heresy in the Church of England was impossible, would it be heresy in an Anglican to deny the existence of God?

ARCHDEACON CHASUBLE, who rose with an air of weariness and languor, would certainly venture to say that if the Church had never been infallible, there was no difficulty in replying to the question proposed by Dr. Easy. If there were no infallible judge to appeal to, there could be no infallible truth; and if there were no infallible truth, it was hard to see how there could be a God, or at least such a God as the Christian religion supposed, who was solicitous about the children of men, and graciously yearned to reveal Himself to them. How, he would ask, could there be a God, —or, to put it more reverently, how could there be a revelation from God to man,—unless there existed a living authority upon earth to teach man infallibly what that revelation was? If men might believe, or were so unfavourably constituted that they *must* believe, many different things about God, or about His truth; either such errors were of no importance, and a matter of perfect indifference to the Most High, or else they were forced to admit that there might be *many* truths, that is, many Gods. For this reason, he had always maintained that Protestantism could only be true on one of three hypotheses: either that there was no God, and therefore no truth; or, secondly, many Gods, and therefore many truths; or, lastly, one God, who either cared nothing about His creatures, or was incapable of securing the execution of His own promises to them, or was of such inconstant variety of purpose that He was continually changing His own views about truth, and never remained in the same mind for twenty years together.

He concluded, therefore, that to deny the existence of an infallible Church, and to deny the existence of the God of Christians, were virtually equivalent propositions. The notion of a fallible church, founded by an infallible God, was an absurdity and a contradiction; such a notion reduced Christianity below the level of the Indian or Chinese systems of religious philosophy, and made it a dispensation of anarchy and chaos. Truth could not rebuke error, because, as had been abundantly proved, there was no such thing as truth or error, and no possibility of distinguishing between them even if they existed. The Protestant theory ingeniously suppressed all heresy, by suppressing the *authority*, the rejection of which constituted heresy. Treason could have no existence where there was no magistrate to rebel against. In the same way, the fallible Church invented by the Reformers was simply a Club for speculative religionists, who were determined to enjoy every privilege of heresy, without incurring the odium of it. If, therefore, the Christian Church were not infallible, he could not resist the logical conclusion that there was no God; for that God was no true God who could send a Teacher to the nations, and an interpreter of His own revelation, as human, as earthly, and as fallible as that House of Convocation itself. (Sensation.)

DR. CANDOUR ventured to solicit the attention of his colleagues while he attempted to reply to the discourse which they had just heard. It was known to most of them that he belonged neither to the High nor the Low-Church party; and on this account he could speak impartially of both. In addressing himself to his task, he would endeavor, by every effort of which he was capable, to clear his mind of the feelings of amazement and stupefaction which the speech of the Archdeacon had created. It was not an easy thing to do, but he would honestly make the attempt.

He respected every sincere conviction, and therefore he respected a conscientious Roman Catholic; but it really seemed to him that for a Protestant to talk about infallibility was an event as wonderful and unexpected as if a Catholic should appeal to the Court of Arches, or an Algerian marabout should submit his conscience to the guidance of an English quaker. However, since they must needs talk of infallibility, let them see what they could make of it.

Now, he must confess, at the outset, that the doctrine "once infallible, always infallible," appeared to him one of the most certain conclusions of common sense. If it was difficult to believe that a Church should *begin* to be infallible which had not been so before, it was impossible to admit that a Church should *cease* to be infallible which had ever been so, even for a moment. Such a gift could only come from God, and, therefore, man could not assume it; it could only be imparted because *necessary* to the Church, and, therefore, God could not withdraw it. But it was demonstrable, according to the Archdeacon, that the Primitive Church was infallible; therefore she was infallible at the time of the Reformation, and therefore the Reformers were children of Satan, and rebels against the Most High. His venerable friend, if he interpreted his looks rightly, appeared to concur in that statement.

But the Archdeacon had assured them that this magnificent gift of infallibility, though lost to the world for the present, might some day be recovered. Before they permitted themselves to contemplate its recovery, let them unite in deploring its loss. It was a hard lot to live in an age when the infallible had become the fallible. He did not know what the existing generation had done to deserve it. He could not help thinking it was a defective arrangement that infallibility should have existed in the purest ages, when Christians were of "one heart and one mind," and, consequently, had less need of it; and that it should be withdrawn at a period of general strife and confusion, when its presence would be so very useful. But, as the Archdeacon had observed, it was their lot to be surrounded by difficulties.

One consolation, however, he was willing to allow them,—the hope that this gift might be recovered. When the Roman, Greek, and Anglican communities should all become one, the Church would be once more infallible. Three spurious and defective Christianities fused together, if anybody could persuade them to coalesce, would make one true and perfect Christianity. The giving up what each believed specially true, and the uniting in what each believed specially false, was that travail in the womb of Christendom which would give birth to the new infallibility. He would only say, as the Professor of Theology had disposed of that point, that this was an obstetrical phenomenon which he did not think any one present would live long enough to witness.

But, he would now approach another aspect of the question, to which the Archdeacon had attracted their attention. The Low-Church theory, he had told them, and the language of their Articles and Homilies, which assumed the defection of the Catholic Church, "made void the promises of God." Was the Archdeacon quite sure that Low-Churchmen were the real or sole offenders? He thought not. Let him ask his friend whether even the "Diabolical Millennium" of the English Reformers, that dismal interval between the sixth and sixteenth centuries, was a conception more insolently subversive of the promises of God, more fatal to the Catholic idea of a divine, indefectible, and "Teaching Church," than the well-known Anglican conceit, that the Early Church was wholly pure, the Mediæval much less pure, and the Modern quite unworthy of their obedience? Was it really so very respectful to the Catholic idea, of which the Archdeacon claimed to be the advocate, to assert, as he and his party did in every act of their lives, that, in spite of the "promises of God," the only really perfect Church at this hour, protesting at once against Protestant heresies and Popish corruptions, was the little group of Puseyites and Ritualists within the National Establishment? (Great laughter.)

The Archdeacon had reproached the Low-Church school, and the founders of Anglicanism, with making void the promises of God. Let the House consider how the High-Church party interpreted those promises for themselves. According to their theory, the promise to be "always" with the Church applied only to the beginning and the end of her career, but not to the long interval between the two, during which the whole of Christendom was hopelessly sunk in error and corruption. It was curious to see that the High-Church party cordially agreed with ultra-Protestants, that the Catholic Church during long ages had been teaching falsehoods! This was their reverence for "the promises of God!"

Again. The promise to guide the Church into "*all* truth" had reference only to the integrity of truth, *before* the mission of St. Augustine to England, and *after* the publication of the "Tracts for the Times." The twelve hundred years between them, rather a long period in the life of the Church, during which all Christians obstinately believed the supremacy of the Pope, the office of the Mother of God, and the Mystery of Transubstantiation,—doctrines highly offensive to Puseyites,—were merely an unfortunate parenthesis in the faithfulness of God, during which the Catholic idea was lamentably obscured, and God forgot His "promises."

Once more. The promise that the "gates of hell" should "*never*" prevail against the Church meant only, according to the same school, that the principalities of evil, doing active work under the father of lies, should certainly prevail for a good many centuries, but that finally a little sect should rise up in the Church of England, able to discriminate with precision the errors of the Anglican, the Greek, and the Roman Churches, and peacefully to conduct them all to the perfect truth which they had lost, to the unity which they had forfeited, and to a very remarkable and final triumph over the "gates of hell."

Perhaps the House would now be disposed to admit that, in point of vigorous and unflinching Protestantism, there was not much difference between High and Low-Churchmen. (General marks of approval.) Indeed, he was inclined to agree with the learned Professor, that in deliberate and self-conscious hostility to Catholic principles, and especially to the doctrine of a Teaching

Church, High-Churchmen outstripped their rivals of every other Protestant community, and left both English Puritans and Scotch Covenanters far in the rear. There was a certain steadfast malice in *their* warfare against the Catholic Church, which they seemed to treat as a personal enemy, and a certain cold and reflecting abhorrence of her claims, of which the ordinary Protestant was perfectly incapable; and while the Puseyites used language about the glories of "the Bride of Christ," and the "Communion of Saints," which no other Protestants could use, they always ended by making cruel havoc of both, and declining to have any communion whatever with any one but themselves. The Christian Church was certainly infallible, Archdeacon Chasuble assured them, for this was her most essential quality; but somehow it had come to pass, in the lapse of ages, that they, the Puseyites, found it necessary to judge the Church, deny her claims, reprove her errors, and offer to reconstruct her on a new basis. God had failed, but they had come to His assistance. The infallibility of the Universal Church, which was at least an imposing idea, had dwindled by degrees to the infallibility of a few dozen English clergymen, which, he would take leave to say, was simply comical.

But his venerable friend had also informed them that he was a "Catholic." Now, let them compare the definition of this term by the High and Low-Church schools respectively, and say which was the most worthy of their applause. In the Low-Church philosophy, to be a Catholic was to be *in* communion with all with whom you professed to differ; in the High-Church philosophy, it was to be *out* of communion with all with whom you claimed to agree. In the one, it was the harmony of universal differences; in the other, it was the unity of three opposing Churches, two of which despised the third, while each anathematised the other. In the Roman sense, which, at least, was rational and intelligible, it meant the absolute oneness in doctrine and discipline of all the Churches which composed the Catholic communion; in the Puseyite sense, which was irrational and absurd, it was simply the arbitrary classification of a hundred different objects under one name. The Catholicity of Rome might be compared to a *Tree*, which had its roots in every land, and displayed in all the same fruits and the same foliage; the Catholicity of Puseyism was at best an artificial *bouquet* of incongruous vegetable forms, composed of a rose, a cabbage, a tulip, and an onion, tied together by a shoe-string. (Much laughter.)

Resuming the three points to which he had referred,—the promises of God, the infallibility of the Church, and the title of Catholic,—he would say, without hesitation, that if he must accept all three together, it was only in the Roman Church that he should look for such a combination. For if Infallibility were the essential prerogative of a Teaching Church, it could only exist in that Institution which *alone* had always claimed it, both as her gift by promise, and the sole explanation of her triumphs and her perpetuity. It would be the idlest of dreams to search for it in a fractional part of a modern community, which had always disowned and scoffed at it, and which could only account for its own existence on the very rational plea, that the Promises of God had signally failed, and that *it* alone was able to correct the failure.

It only remained for him, in order to exhaust the topics of the Archdeacon's address, to examine, if the House would permit him, that very remarkable doctrine which was generally known as "the Branch-theory." He thought it would not be difficult to show, that if the Archdeacon was a Catholic without Catholicity, he was also a Branch without a Trunk.

His venerable friend, if he might construct a speech for one who was so well able to speak for himself, might be supposed to address the Roman Church as follows:—"I admit that my Church is not, and cannot be, the Church Catholic. I admit, further, that she is not a Church at all, except in a political or national sense. But I contend that, in spite of her defects, she is a *branch* of the Universal Communion, however earnestly you may repudiate the connection; and I insist that I am not excluded from your pale, because I do not recognise your right to exclude me. I claim to determine that point for myself. I choose to belong to you, whether you consent or not. I will not resign my communion with Rome, though I know that you rank me with the aliens outside; and I must positively refuse to enter her communion, though you affectionately entreat me to do so. In a word, I *will* belong to you, in spite of your rejection; and I will *not* obey you in spite of your invitation."

This was the way in which the branch spoke to the trunk

Well, was it really a branch, and if so, on what part of the trunk was it grafted? At what point did the vivifying sap flow from the one to the other? It was easy, of course, to understand the metaphor in the case of a French, a Spanish, or an Austrian clergyman, who believed every doctrine of the Catholic Church, and was in filial subjection to her Head, from whom alone he professed to derive his mission and jurisdiction. Such men were, doubtless, in a very real sense, "branches" of the Roman trunk. But an Anglican, by whatever fancy names he might seek to disguise himself, was simply a child of the Reformation, without which his Church would never have come into existence; and, moreover, that Church began its career by informing the world, through the mouth of all its master-builders, that the Catholic Church was the Babylon of the Apocalypse. How then, once more, could *he* be a branch of the Roman trunk?

He had heard, indeed, of a well-known clergyman, lately deceased, who said to a friend, in answer to the inquiry how they were to establish their connection with the Catholic Church, "May there not be underground suckers?" This was all which the author of the "Christian Year" could suggest to dissuade a brother minister from going over to Rome! But, surely, such idle words could hardly satisfy a man who believed he had a soul. Branches were not connected with a tree by invisible and imaginary suckers, but grew bodily out of its substance. And, moreover, they were always of the same material. He would ask his venerable friend if ever he saw a tree with one branch of oak, another of cypress, and a third of ebony? Did he ever see thistles growing on a vine, or olives on a fig tree? Yet even such a vegetable combination would, in his judgment, be a far less curious *lusus naturæ* than a theological reproduction of the Siamese twins, in the shape of a disciple of the Thirty-Nine Articles locked in the embrace of a pupil of Cardinal Bellarmine.

The only true test of a theory was the result to which it led in practice. The branch-theory did not look well on paper, but perhaps it redeemed itself in its practical evolution? He would suppose, then, that the Archdeacon, resolving to try his theory, set out on a foreign tour. Did he leave Dover an Anglican, and disembark at Calais a Roman Catholic? If so, at what particular spot in the Channel did he drop the Anglican Articles and take up the Roman Missal? Was it marked by a buoy? or was the transformation a gradual process, like the changes of temperature? On leaving Dover he carried with him only two sacraments, which had grown into seven by the time he landed at Calais. Supposing the distance to be twenty-five miles, did he take up a new sacrament, —he was going to say at every fifth milestone, but the sea knew not such measures of distance. Were there fixed points at which he *began* to believe that Transubstantiation was a holy mystery, and not a "blasphemous fable;" that Confirmation and Extreme Unction were divine sacraments, and not, as he had believed while breakfasting at Dover, a mere "corrupt following of the Apostles?" Did he, in spite of the injunction with which they were all familiar, "not to speak to the man at the wheel," anxiously interrogate that individual as to the precise longitude in which it behoved him to cast away some Anglican delusion, and take up some Catholic truth? At what point of the voyage did the Pope's supremacy begin to dawn upon him? And, finally, did the process of transformation, to which all Branch-Christians were inevitably subject when they went to foreign lands, depend in any degree upon the weather? Was it quicker or slower in a heavy sea? or did sea-sickness in any way affect its development?

But he would now suppose that, instead of visiting France or Belgium, or any other Catholic land, his friend should allow himself the recreation of a voyage to the Baltic, and disembark on the banks of the Neva. They were all aware that the "Holy Eastern Church" was just now spoken of with a comically exaggerated reverence by a certain section of the English clergy, whose raptures did not seem to be checked by the discouraging fact that the "Holy Anglican Church" was an institution totally ignored by Greek and Muscovite alike. Mr. Curzon had been asked, a few years ago, by the Patriarch of Constantinople, "who the Archbishop of Canterbury *was*?" The head of the Greek Church had never even heard of him! Now, their friend, the Archdeacon, would carry with him to Russia his principle of branch-churches, which, by hypothesis, would make him everywhere at home; and he would be as much imbued with Russian theology on arriving at St. Petersburg, as he was with Roman on arriving at Calais. He would now consider the "Orthodox" religion at least as good as the "Catholic," if not a great deal better. The Papal supremacy, equally odious to him and to the Russian, would become once more a "usurpation," and the Czar would henceforth be his Pontiff, not the Pope. Imperial maxims would penetrate his mind; and the violent destruction of Catholic interests in Poland and in Lithuania would claim his warm approval, as in Calais it excited his horror and disgust. The transformation of this Branch-Christian would be once more radical and complete! He changed his religion with as much facility as he changed his coat. The fact that English, Roman, and Russian creeds were so distinct as to involve perpetual and deadly schism, only rendered his conversion to all three by turns a greater stretch of Christian charity. If *they* did not know how to agree with one another, *he* knew how to agree with all of them; so that the Archdeacon appeared to have adopted this new theological formula, that "the impartial distribution of mutual anathemas was the truest condition of mutual communion."

One difficulty, however, would await him at St. Petersburg, from which he was exempt at Calais. It was true that neither at Calais nor at St. Petersburg would he meet a single priest who would regard him as anything but a heretic and a schismatic. In Russia, as in France, none would consent to join him in the simple act of worship, in spite of his provisional assumption of the Russian Creed. But, then, it was a fact well-known in Russia, that the Greek Church had been often reconciled to Rome, and always upon terms imposed upon her by the latter; and had often admitted, as at the Council of Florence, that the Pope was the Vicar of God. So that the Archdeacon would have changed his doctrine, and changed again, only to find at last that the truth which he had abhorred at Dover, and confessed at Calais, and abhorred once more in Russia, in order to enjoy everywhere the privilege of being a "Branch-Christian," was just as well appreciated in Russia as in Rome, was actually enshrined in her liturgies, and only denied by the former, at the present day, on political grounds, because it presented the most formidable obstacle to Slavonic national unity. Was it worth while, then, to maintain a theory which would not secure for him the faintest recognition by any Church throughout the world; which required its advocate to show even less respect for *positive* truth than the Mormon or the Kaffir; and which far from attracting the sympathy of the Greek or Roman Churches, which it was foolishly designed to conciliate, only united them both in common and undisguised contempt?

And here he would briefly narrate an incident which occurred not many years ago, in illustration of the folly of the branch-religion. An Anglican clergyman desired to receive the sacrament at St. Petersburg. He was told, among other things, that he must first anathematise the Thirty-Nine Articles. He replied, as Archdeacon Chasuble might do, that he was quite prepared to do so. On this his Russian friends, who thought Branch-Christians simply a nuisance, and only wanted to get rid of him, observed that more was necessary, and that he must bring a solemn declaration from *all* the Anglican bishops, that they also anathematised the Articles. It would certainly be a remarkable day on which the collective Anglican Episcopate should declare their own Church accursed, as these Russians politely proposed; and as the clergyman in question was not sanguine that he could persuade them to do so, he gave it up, and went to Constantinople to be admitted into the Greek Church. But there they rudely informed him that he must be re-baptized, to which he strongly objected. Once more he travelled to St. Petersburg, where they told him the ecclesiastics at Constantinople were ignorant boobies, at which he opened his eyes very wide indeed, and finished by becoming a Roman Catholic; in which condition he wished him all possible felicity.

But he would detain the House no longer; and as the Archdeacon had concluded his discourse by showing how, on *his* principles, Dr. Easy's principles should be answered, he would beg permission to follow his example. It was his opinion, then, that if the Branch-idea be true, there must be *three* Gods, and not one; and each of them on such deplorable terms with the other two, that it was a marvel how Olympus could contain them without a general celestial catastrophe.

DEAN PRIMITIVE must really protest against such unbecoming levity.

DR. CANDOUR could assure the Dean that he never was more serious in his life. If there was any touch of levity or comedy in the discussion, it was in the subject and not in his treatment of it. He would go farther, and say that either indignation or contempt must be provoked in every honest mind by the modern theory which he had attempted to refute. He insisted that that theory required the existence of three distinct and hostile gods,—an Anglican, a Greek, and a Roman; and that on any disputed point of doctrine an English clergyman would only have to say *which* of the three he proposed to serve, in order effectually to puzzle the Privy Council, and keep himself safe from the imputation of heresy. He was brought, therefore, to the same conclusion as his venerable friend. If to deny the infallibility of the Church, as he maintained, was the same with denying the existence of a God,—because God could not possibly establish a fallible Church,—it was equally certain that to suppose *three* warring and wrangling Churches, all teaching different doctrines, yet all protected and commissioned by one common Founder, and regarded by him with equal complacency, was to admit that there were three Gods; and this was the same with saying that there was no God at all. And thus, by different roads, he and his friend the Archdeacon arrived at precisely the same conclusion.

THE PROLOCUTOR of the House here rose, with an air of dignity becoming his official character, and expressed his conviction that the general feeling of the House was that the debate should now close. (Hear, hear.) That debate had proved a variety of things, which were more or less destructive to the National Church, but nothing perhaps more clearly than this, that the public was right in regarding their discussions as very unprofitable to the interests of religion, either in their own land or in any other. He did not see what was gained by showing the world that no two of them were of the same mind, and that Convocation had no more authority to lead men to the truth than the Church which it was supposed to represent. He thought, indeed, the time had come when Convocation should cease to meet as a representative body, affecting to deal with interests which it had no power to promote, and to serve a cause which it was only able to compromise. Its deliberations,—which might have a certain value if they pretended to no official character,—were now regarded by everbody as a sham, and probably their own convictions were in harmony with that view. He proposed, therefore, that this should be the last official meeting of Convocation,—(Loud cheers,)—and that henceforth they should assemble in the house of one of their colleagues, where they could converse together freely, like any other private company, without the risk of exciting public animadversion. He really thought that a few more meetings of Convocation would destroy the Church of England altogether, since the only dogma which that body could be said to have defined was this, that "Christianity, from first to last, was entirely a matter of opinion;" whereas, in their private capacity, they could discuss every point of Christian doctrine, without suggesting the idea to thoughtful minds that the primary object of the Christian revelation was to make it impossible for any man to know the truth. If the House shared his opinion, it only remained to determine what should be the place of their future meeting. (Applause.)

DR. EASY was delighted to be able to offer hospitality to his reverend friends. He lived, as they knew, in the immediate neighbourhood of their fine old historical abbey, and his apartments were sufficiently spacious to afford a convenient place of meeting. He proposed, therefore, on the understanding that Convocation was now happily extinct, that they should meet at his residence on that day week, when they could either resume the debate that had hitherto occupied them, or turn their attention to any other topic which might promise greater profit or amusement. (Loud cries of "Agreed.")

[*Exeunt omnes.*]

SCENE II.

DR. EASY'S DRAWING-ROOM.

DR. EASY's drawing-room presented an animated appearance. Friendly greetings were exchanged, and decent hilarity pervaded the assembly. The gravest countenances relaxed from conventional severity. Archdeacons smiled as if in anticipation of coming enjoyment, and even Deans responded to the salutations of the inferior clergy with unwonted urbanity. The bright mirrors, well-selected pictures, and far-reaching sofas which adorned Dr. Easy's saloon, and bore witness at once to the amplitude of his revenues and the refinement of his taste, were evidently felt to be an improvement on the decorous gloom of the Jerusalem Chamber. Tables of marble and rosewood were covered with choice engravings and other works of art. Portraits of the Misses Easy attracted the attention of the younger clergy. The absence of reporters imparted to their elder brethren a welcome sense of liberty. Free, but not undignified, postures preluded the familiar dialogue in which each could take cheerful part, without the unpleasant fear of newspaper criticism. Convocation had become a social or family reunion, and was evidently satisfied with the change. Informal discussion preceded the coming debate, and themes which never fail to interest the clerical mind occupied the company. Dean Pompous disputed with a neighbour the exact pecuniary value of a benefice likely to be shortly vacant, and suggested a probable successor to the dying incumbent. Dean Primitive conversed with Archdeacon Chasuble on the recent letter of the Primate, inviting the Bishops "in visible communion with the Church of England" to a Council in September. Had his friend noticed, he asked, that remarkable announcement that "such Council would *not* be competent to make declarations, or lay down definitions on points of doctrine?" His friend had certainly noticed it. He had heard of Councils, both general and local, which had assembled to *decide* on points of doctrine, but it was the first time he had ever heard of a Council summoned with the avowed object of *avoiding* all such questions. In such cheerful talk the reverend guests continued to indulge, till their number being at length complete, there arose suddenly, amid the hum of general conversation, a loud cry of "Chair, chair!" Then the host, leaning against a chimney-piece, bowed to his friends, and prayed them to be seated. Silence being restored, the debate commenced as follows:—

DR. EASY rejoiced that his reverend friends had attended in such imposing numbers. In compliance with their invitation, he had selected a subject to be submitted to their notice. Their last debate, as they seemed generally to feel, had proved to themselves and to the public that Authority neither did nor could reside in the English Church. It was certain that no individual clergyman, nor all the clergy put together, could decide any point of doctrine whatever; so that the day seemed close at hand,—if it had not actually arrived,—when an Anglican would be at liberty either to accept or reject every truth contained in the Christian revelation. The learned Prolocutor had well epitomised all the points of their last debate, and gracefully justified the characteristic decisions of Privy Council, when he said, or at least implied, that the practical result of all Anglican teaching, as of all Anglican history, might be expressed in such a formula as this: "Christianity, from first to last, is simply a matter of opinion;" or, "The primary object of the Christian Revelation is to render it impossible for any man to know the truth with certainty."

In confirmation of this view of their position as members of the Established Church, he was happy to be able to call their attention to the recent declaration of one of her highest dignitaries. He regretted that he was not present with them, that he might have enforced in person the very striking statements which he was about to quote from a published volume of his sermons, with which he (Dr. Easy) had only become acquainted since their last meeting. The very Rev. Dr. Elliot, the present Dean of Bristol, had publicly asserted, without incurring the slightest shadow of reproach, these two momentous truths; (1) that the Church of England is, in all respects, a purely human institution; and (2) that her members are not bound in conscience to believe a single doctrine taught by her. But he would quote his exact words:

"The Church of England," said the Dean of Bristol, "is created by the law, upheld by the law, paid by the law, and may be changed by the law, *just as any other institution in the land.*"

That was his first proposition, and here was the second:

"I cannot desire you to accept either what I affirm, or what the Church affirms, as undoubtedly true, or *the only true* interpretation of the mysteries of God."

It was pleasant to see the conclusions at which they had arrived in a former debate embraced with so much energy of conviction by one of the highest functionaries of their National Church. And now, accepting these conclusions as indisputable, and harmonising perfectly with the life and history of that Church, he was led to ask; "If the Authority of the English Church be purely human, can her Orders be divine?" This was the question he should propose for their consideration, and without another word of preface, he would submit the following motion to their vote:—"That this meeting, being unanimous on the point that Authority can have no existence in the Church of England, desires to pass to the discussion of the cognate question, 'ARE ENGLISH ORDERS HUMAN OR DIVINE?'"

(The motion being carried by show of hands, Dr. Easy invited the Professor of History to open the debate, on the ground that no one was more qualified to handle the subject, and to discriminate with accuracy the delicate considerations connected with it.)

THE PROFESSOR OF HISTORY rose from an ottoman, and then, in compliance with a general request, stood upon it, for the convenience of his hearers. He had naturally, he said, given some attention to a subject on which it had been his duty to lecture to the students of one of the Universities. In earlier years, before he accepted the responsibility of teaching others, he had been accustomed to maintain the validity of English Orders to his own satisfaction by some such process as the following: "There can be no orders without Apostolic Succession, therefore it follows that *we* must possess it." He need hardly observe that his maturer reason rejected this crude argumentation,—(laughter)—but it pained him to be obliged to add, that too many of the clergy at the present day employed logical methods quite as feeble and inconclusive as that which he had renounced. Their reasoning on this important subject, involving intricate points of history as well as moral difficulties of a very serious kind, was often trivial and childish, quite unworthy of the gravity of the subject, and only tending to throw discredit upon it. He should be glad if he could induce them to adopt a more manly tone, and perhaps he could not better illustrate his meaning than by suggesting the following cautions, by way of example.

Thus, with respect to the Ordinal of Edward VI., which had been recently discussed in certain public journals, he could not seriously advise his reverend friends to argue that, because that form was *new*, it was therefore necessarily Catholic. Nor, because it did *not* contain one word of Episcopal consecration, must it therefore have been efficient to the making of a bishop. Nor, because it was annulled in the reign of Queen Mary, must it therefore have been legal in that of Elizabeth. Nor, because Queen Elizabeth, labouring under the temporary impression that she was Almighty God, "*dispensed* with all causes and doubts of any imperfection of the same," should he therefore conclude that that dispensation was straightway ratified in Heaven. Nor, once more, because Charles II., one hundred and twelve years after the new form began to be used, pronounced it invalid by substituting another in its place, should he therefore attribute to that royal but light-minded pontiff, the omnipotence which he claimed in his turn, nor admit his power to unite the links of a succession which his own act declared to have been hopelessly broken.

In the same way, if he were discussing that *vexata quæstio*, the consecration of Archbishop Parker, he would not press the argument too closely, that, because the register of his consecration was not discovered for half a century, the fact was clearly providential, and involved a *primâ facie* probability that Parker was a true bishop. Nor, again, because the register of Barlow's consecration, who was said to have consecrated Parker, was never discovered at all, should he therefore insist that *his* consecration attained to a point of demonstration which was akin to absolute certainty.

In like manner, when he considered the historical fact, that most of the Reformers, especially those who had the principal influence in determining the tone of their formularies, openly despised the rite of Ordination, he could not counsel his brethren to attribute to them a delicate fastidiousness in their mode of administering it, which they would certainly have disowned with scorn. Thus, because Barlow was known to have regarded Ordination as a trifling and impertinent thing, declaring that "any *layman* whom the king might choose to be a bishop, would be as good a bishop as himself, or the best in England;" he should not from that fact infer that Barlow was likely to be painfully scrupulous in his own mode of consecrating a bishop, or that his estimate of the imposition of hands was quite identical with that of Archdeacon Chasuble. Nor, again, because Coverdale and Scorey, the co-ordainers of Parker, were lively and recreative monks, who, along with Barlow, had broken into shivers their voluntary vows of chastity, in order to embrace delights from which they had bound their souls to abstain, was he therefore driven imperiously to the conviction, that they *must* have been inflexible on the point of their Orders, to compensate for the deficiency on the score of their morality. Nor, once more, because Scorey and Barlow had been Catholics *and* Protestants under Henry, Catholics again under Mary, and Protestants once more under Elizabeth; should he therefore attribute to either of those versatile prelates a fanatical attachment to religion in general, or to the exact administration of holy Orders in particular.

All which was known of the other Reformers furnished a motive for exercising similar caution with respect to *their* opinions of the Apostolic Succession. Because Cranmer contended before all England that "the King's election alone, *without* ordination, sufficed to make a priest or a bishop;" or because *thirteen* other bishops subscribed the formal declaration that "bishops and priests are *not* two things, but one office in the beginning of Christ's religion;" or because Whittaker bluntly requested his Roman Catholic assailants to "keep their Orders to themselves;" or because Fulke, with **even** greater emphasis, described those Orders, as "*stinking, greasy, and anti-Christian;*" or because Jewel declined three times to answer Harding's taunting question, "Who made *you* a bishop?" or, finally, because Parker, Jewel, and Horne combined together in their version of the Bible to translate χειροvoυια "ordination by *election*," which translation remained till the time of James I.: he could not, from all such facts, conclude that integrity of Holy Order was the grand passion of the first fathers of the English Church, or, indeed, that they regarded it with any less aversion than purgatory or the confession of their sins.

It had been argued, by their High-Church brethren, in order to take the sting out of such facts, that the early Anglican bishops were in mortal fear of the brutal Tudor sovereigns, and would have been in their own views, and have made the Anglican formularies, much more Catholic, if they had been free to follow their private aspirations. But such a trifling allegation was equally at variance with reason and with history. If the English bishops sacrificed their own convictions of truth from cowardice,—as this theory wantonly assumed,—they were pitiful traitors; and the Church, which such men founded, had very little claim to their respect. But, in fact, it was the strong will of the Tudor sovereigns which alone prevented the bishops from being still *more* Protestant than they actually were. But for that fierce temper which brooked no opposition, it was impossible to doubt that the Church of England would have been framed in closer accordance with a Genevan model; and if this had not come to pass, it was certainly not to the bishops that their thanks were due. The Stuarts also so far resembled the Tudors that, owing to their notions of kingly prerogative, they were willing to retain certain Catholic traditions which the English clergy and people valued much less than their rulers. They owed to kings, and not to bishops, whatever superficial distinctions separated them from the non-Episcopal Protestant communities.

It would be noticed that in the observations which he had made thus far, he had expressed no personal opinion as to the validity of English Orders. He had merely suggested prudence and caution in dealing with arguments which, however indecisive they might appear, when taken one by one, possessed a certain cumulative force which was not to be despised. They might have weight, but they were not conclusive, either one way or the other. In like manner, the fact that Roman Catholics treated their Orders as purely human, however serious it might be in conjunction with other facts which he would notice presently, could hardly by itself be deemed decisive on the point. Roman Catholics were their natural enemies, and might be mistaken as to matters of fact, or unduly biassed in their appreciation of them.

DEAN PRIMITIVE, who appeared to listen to the Professor with extreme dissatisfaction, wished to inquire, if he might be allowed to interrupt the speaker, whether the hostile *animus* of the Roman Church towards the Church of England was not distinctly proved by the fact that she made no difficulty in recognising the Orders of the modern Russia, nor even of the Jacobite, Coptic, and other oriental communities?

THE PROFESSOR interpreted that fact in exactly the opposite sense. The Orders of the communities referred to by the Dean had *never* been disputed, while their own had never been admitted, by any religious body on the face of the earth. But he preferred to examine the question in connection with general principles, rather than with reference to particular and isolated facts.

Now, he found it laid down by certain writers, with an emphasis which showed the importance they attributed to it, that wherever the mystical doctrines of the Sacrifice of the Altar and the Real Presence, of which hardly anything had ever been heard in their own Church until the last few years, had been retained in any Christian community, *there*, whatever might have been their destiny in other respects, no question as to the integrity of their Orders had ever arisen. It was only, they urged, in communions like the English, where those doctrines had been *rejected* as "fables" and "deceits," and where, in practice, they had been quite put out of sight for centuries, that the proofs of what was called the Apostolic Succession were not found. His friends would admit that, at least from a Catholic point of view, which some of their colleagues were fond of adopting, this was a fact of tremendous gravity. He was not surprised that to many minds it seemed absolutely decisive of the whole question. They argued, with great force on their own principles, that such a Church as the English, which had pronounced by the mouth of its founders, by the testimony of its formularies, and by the practice of three centuries, that the doctrines in question were false, could not possibly share the Succession with communions which had always revered them as true. They insisted, and he thought with reason, that the Christian priesthood and the mysteries of the altar were correlatives, and that they must stand or fall together. This was no special doctrine of the Roman Church. It was held by East and West alike, that the peculiar doctrinal statements, and still more the uniform practice of the English Church, were absolutely inconsistent with the possibility of sacerdotal powers; and the same objectors observed that, as a matter of fact, notably confirming this view, the English was the solitary Episcopal communion in which the proofs of the succession were not to be had, or had always been rejected as insufficient.

But they said a great deal more than this. Their High-Church friends,—having acquired by study an intellectual conviction of the truth of certain Catholic doctrines, utterly repudiated in practice by their co-religionists,—were anxious to prove that such doctrines were admitted, or at least not rejected, by the National Church. They claimed to be priests, with all the powers which had ever been supposed to accompany the sacerdotal office. To this claim their adversaries replied, that supposing for the sake of argument, they *had* these powers, then was the history of their community one long unbroken calendar of crime and sacrilege, as well as of lying teaching against the doctrines of the Catholic Church. The very first act, they observed, of the Reformed Church of England was to suspend, if not to abolish, the daily sacrifice, and to substitute in its place the occasional celebration of a rite which had nothing in common with it but the use of bread and wine. It was noticed with regret by some of the early Anglican bishops, that in many Churches communion was hardly given "*once in three months,*" so utterly had all notion of the Christian Sacrifice disappeared! What they then lamented had since become, until the last few years, the almost *universal* rule in every part of England. If, therefore, as the Ritualists maintained, the daily sacrifice was the essential rite of the Christian religion, it was undeniable that their own Church was *an apostate community*, since she had suffered that rite to lapse, without an effort to restore it, during three centuries. And in this course she did but follow the teaching of her founders. The greatest English prelates, including Ridley, ordered every Catholic altar to be pulled down and utterly defaced; some of them commanding that the very altar-stones should be placed at the entrance to the churches, so that all who entered should be *forced* to tread upon them.* The altar was treated

---

* Here a Reverend Divine handed to his neighbour the following extracts, which he appeared to carry about his person as charms or relics, with this emphatic observation: "See how the Court of Arches and the Privy Council have caught the spirit of our admirable Reformers, the sainted founders of the Anglican Church!"

CRANMER. "The Papists teach that Christ is in the bread and wine; but *we* say (according to the truth) that He is in them that worthily eat and drink the bread and wine."—*Answer to Gardner*, 3rd Book, p. 52. Again; "Presence by faith only meaneth *no real*, material, and corporal presence. For by faith is Christ present *in baptism*,—and the holy fathers did eat His flesh and drink His blood *before he was born*."—*Against Transubstantiation*, 2nd Book, p. 296.

RIDLEY, in giving a reason for taking down and removing the Catholic altars, said: "The use of an *altar* is to make sacrifice upon it; the use of a *table*," which he ordered to be everywhere substituted, "is to serve for men to eat upon."—*Injunction*, p. 322. "It is not read that any of the Apostles or the Primitive Church did ever use any *altar* in ministration of the holy communion." p. 323.

LATIMER: "*Minister* is a more fit name than priest, for the name of a priest importeth a *sacrifice*."—*Disputation at Oxford*, p. 264. Again, "Christ gave not His body to be received with the mouth; . . . He gave the sacrament to the mouth, His body *to the mind*," p. 267. "I could never find," he adds, with bitter mockery of the Real Presence, "in the sacrament of the body and blood of Christ, (which the Papists call the sacrament of the *altar*,) neither flesh, blood, nor bones."

BECON, Cranmer's favourite chaplain, knowing the whole mind of the Anglican Reformers, said: "The Papists have brought in their bloody and butcherly *altars*."—*The Supplication*, p. 229. He reproaches God for suffering them to say "their idolatrous and devilish masses." He reviles "Antichrist's (the Pope's) blasphemous masses, his idolatrous *altars*, his *carish confession*," &c. "The sacraments of the new law," he adds, "*do not confer and give grace*."—*Articles of Christian Religion*, 16th Article, p. 466.

JEWEL: "The body of Christ is to be eaten by faith only, *and none otherwise*."—*Answer to Harding*, p. 449.

HOOPER: "Baptism sanctifieth no man."—*A Declaration of Christ and His Office*, p. 74. "The Jews had sacraments as well as we, and yet never brawled about them as we do." p. 211. "There should, among Christians, be *no altars*."

GRINDAL ordered all altars to be utterly removed, and, in place of the rood, to put up "some convenient crest."—*Articles for the Province of Canterbury*, p. 158.

Such was the theology of the founders of the Anglican Church, faithfully interpreted by the decisions of the Privy Council.

in England, under her Reformers, as the Cross was in Japan. And why? Evidently, because the eminent and sagacious men to whom they owed their present religious *status* knew perfectly well that, if they could get rid of the altar, they should have no difficulty in abolishing the sacrifice. The event proved that they were right. They *did* abolish it, and every idea connected with it. And, on this account, he thought that Puseyites should earnestly hope that their Orders could not be the same with those of Rome. They should prefer to think *themselves* deluded, rather than attribute hideous crimes to the great majority of those who ministered in their communion. For, considering the manner in which the Lord's Supper had notoriously been administered for centuries, even in their cathedrals, and much more in parish churches, almost every celebration in the Church of England, from the time of Queen Elizabeth to their own, had been simply, *supposing the Catholic doctrine to be true,* an appalling outrage on the Person of the Son of God. Let them call to mind the details, often absolutely grotesque, of such celebrations in their English communion, and they would recoil with horror from the results of their own theory, which implied a long series of sacrileges so utterly monstrous and incredible, that the mind refused to contemplate them.

His friend, Dean Primitive, suggested that the Church of Rome had some sinister motive in repudiating Anglican orders. Yet here was a motive, quite independent of all historical difficulties, which was surely sufficient to the Catholic mind! The Church of Rome had never been in the habit of denying true Orders where they really existed. There were many Christian bodies in their own day, as in past ages, vehemently hostile to the Roman Church, but whose Orders she never dreamed of disputing. The Arians had true Orders, so had the Donatists, the Nestorians, and a multitude of other sects; but it was worthy to be carefully noted by their High-Church friends, that in all their combats with the Latin Church, they never once pleaded them! There was literally no example in ecclesiastical history, previous to the formation of the English Church, of any controversy on the subject of Orders. Questions of *doctrine* only, up to the sixteenth century, had ever been debated between the rival Churches. It was reserved for English Protestant theologians to give a singular and suspicious prominence to this topic of Orders. Their adversaries would probably say, that the explanation of this curious fact was easy to find. They would see in it only a fresh proof that the Reformation, having destroyed all *positive* truth, by proclaiming the right of every individual to determine truth for himself, had made all controversies about doctrine utterly illogical and unmeaning, and had left nothing to dispute about, to those who cared to dispute at all, but the question of Protestant Orders.

He had already observed, and would again affirm, in a spirit of fairness to the Roman Church, which would deem herself convicted of sacrilege if she repeated knowingly the ordination of a true priest, that she was not alone in rejecting English Orders, nor in regarding them as a purely civil privilege, conferred under the sanction of English law. They were equally rejected, when pretending to any higher character than this, by every other Christian community in the world. Even the obscure little Syrian body in Western India, when solicited by the Bishop of Calcutta to fraternise with Anglicans, scornfully derided them. How was it possible, he would ask, to resent or marvel at such judgments, when a majority of their own clergy, at all epochs had agreed with the present Dean of Bristol, that the question was too unreal and fantastic to be treated with a grave deliberation? "The 25th Article," as the Dean truly observed, "*denies* that Orders are a Sacrament…. In contradiction to Rome, it clearly repudiated it *as a fiction altogether*, that God had annexed peculiar grace and authority to imposition of hands successively from the apostles, or to any other arbitrary form of ordination whatever."

It was evident, then, as every intelligent person would admit, that the validity of English Orders was not, as Ritualists were pleased to maintain, a solemn controversy between the English and the Roman Churches. It was, to speak with truth and candour, a dispute in which a small section of their own community was on one side, and the whole of Christendom on the other. Let his younger friends remember, that when they innocently supposed they were bravely pleading their Orders against the cruel Church of Rome, (which would anathematise them quite as heartily if their Orders were perfectly indisputable,) they were, in fact, engaged in the much more difficult task of defending them against the *orbis terrarum*, with no sympathy from any Christian alive or dead, not even from the few Protestant communities which were in precisely the same dilemma as themselves.

DEAN PRIMITIVE, who rose with an air of radiant triumph, exclaimed, that the Professor was evidently going a great deal too far, since several distinguished Romanists had candidly admitted the validity of Anglican Orders. ("Hear, hear," from some of the younger clergy.)

THE PROFESSOR had carefully tested the value of all the witnesses referred to, and was afraid they would not afford much consolation to the Dean. There was Courayer, who wanted to vex the community from which he was already falling away, and who at last died an infidel. His friend was welcome to his testimony. There was Bossuet, who certainly said of the validity of English Orders, "*cela depend des faits*," as the Pope himself would be the first to admit; but when the Abbé Le Grand asked him whether he might without offence style Burnet "Bishop of Salisbury," tersely replied, "*Nous ne connaissons pas cet episcopat là.*" This was very flattering to English Orders. Dr. Lingard also had been cited as admitting, with more or less hesitation, the purely historical side of the question of Parker's consecration. But such half-admissions, on the part of a few individuals, proved nothing whatever, and could not possibly outweigh the *consensus* of all the Christian churches, and their actual conduct towards all orders of the English clergy. He knew that some of his friends professed to see the hand of Providence in the fact, that the Council of Trent had not expressly condemned their Orders. They were perhaps not aware that the Council was within an inch of doing so, and was only restrained by a most urgent appeal from the Spanish ambassador, who represented that the condition of English Catholics was already nearly intolerable, and that the superfluous declaration would only irritate their oppressors, and bring fresh misery upon them. This argument wisely prevailed. But there was to be a new Council next year, and, from information which had reached him, he had not a shadow of doubt that it would not only decide *that* point, but a good many others which his High-Church friends were extremely anxious to keep open. There was evidently sorrow and trouble in store for them, and their position would soon be more untenable than ever.

He had detained the company too long, but would ask permission, in conclusion, to express his own belief that the historical aspect of the question of their Orders, whatever difficulties might belong to it, and though it was absolutely certain that it could never be decided now in their favour, was of comparatively little importance. Even if Parker's ordination could be proved, and Edward's Ordinal cleared of every doubt, and a multitude of other questions connected with the subject lose their gravity, no progress would have been made towards establishing the claims of the *present* generation of bishops and clergy. *Their* case was still worse than that of Elizabeth's much afflicted spiritual pastors. The extreme uncertainty of Baptism during the whole of the Puritan period, to speak only of that epoch; nay, the positive contempt in which that sacrament was held by whole generations of English Protestant divines, and the utter indifference with which it was administered; the want of intention in hundreds of consecrating bishops to *confer* sacerdotal powers, and in thousands of the clergy to *accept* them; the alleged fact that at least one Archbishop of Canterbury was known to have died unbaptized, and the extreme probability that many others had been in the same case; lastly, the outrageous incongruity of pretending to make a *Catholic* bishop, as the Ritualists spoke, out of a man who rejected all Catholic doctrine, and spent his whole life in reviling it; these were graver subjects of reflection to those who affected to derive English Orders from the Roman fount, than any merely historical difficulties. And when the two were combined, they certainly sufficed to justify both the Latin and Greek communities in sternly rejecting, as a fable and a pretence, the claim of a few Anglican ministers to be true priests.

It was a wholesome maxim in all controversy to be as fair to your adversary as the infirmities of human nature would permit. It would not contribute to a mutual understanding quietly to ignore all his strong points. In this case of English Orders they were both numerous and formidable. They had first to prove that Parker was really consecrated; then to consider whether Barlow had either the will or the power to consecrate him. Next, to account for the fact that all England believed the whole thing was a sham, which Elizabeth's characteristic decree frankly confessed, by trying to *repair* it; and that the bishops were of the same opinion, since they evidently felt that, if the Queen could do nothing for them, their case was hopeless. Then they must deal with the fact, that all the Reformers, and their immediate successors, were not only ill-affected towards the Apostolic Succession, but did every thing they could to discredit it; clearly proving that they neither attached any importance to it, nor imagined that they themselves possessed it. They must reconcile their deep hatred of the doctrine of sacrifice with their ordination of a priesthood, whose chief function it was to offer sacrifice. They must explain also why, if Edward's Ordinal were valid, Anglicans need have been so anxious to change it, a hundred years after it had become too late to do so with any possible result. They must refute, when they had accomplished these preliminary difficulties, the really irresistible reasons for believing that a vast number of English bishops and clergy must have lived and died unbaptized, and were therefore perfectly incapable either of receiving or giving ordination, or any other Christian rite. And when they had arranged all these points to their own satisfaction, they would have to consider, finally, what object Providence could have in view in creating whole generations of "priests," who neither wished to be so, nor believed that they were, nor ever consciously performed one single act belonging to the sacerdotal office!

On the whole, they were perhaps now disposed to admit, that the Church of Rome was neither capricious nor unjust, when she admitted a Protestant bishop into her communion, just as if he had been all his life a layman. First conditionally baptized, then unconditionally confirmed, his diaconate, priesthood, and episcopate all went for nothing. The Anglican bishop, Gordon, and the American bishop, Ives, who were reconciled to the Church of Rome, were dealt with in this way, and no more respect was paid to their former ecclesiastical character than if they had both been women. If the Archbishop of Canterbury were to become a Catholic to-morrow, an event which they had no reason to anticipate, he would be welcomed by the Roman Church as an English married gentleman, who was tired of playing a farce, and had come to save his soul in the Christian Church. Such was the fact. It was truly, then, a marvel that any Anglicans should gravely talk of "union" with Rome, or conceive that it was possible, except on the condition of absolute submission to all ner claims. Let his High-Church friends look to this. It was a mere voluntary delusion to blind themselves to the fact, which every day made clearer, that the Roman Church cared no more what were their private opinions as to what is "Catholic," and what is not, and allowed them to exert no more influence upon her acts, than their views on the polarization of light, or the character of Napoleon, or the possibility of making a tunnel under the English Channel.

DR. EASY thought he might venture to say, on behalf of the company, that they were grateful to the Professor for the very interesting observations he had made. If he were allowed to resume them in a single sentence, this was the conclusion he should draw from them; that the clergy of their national community deserved the esteem which they enjoyed, and rendered services which the country was not disposed to undervalue; but that their Orders were simply human, and had no shadow of pretence to any supernatural character. They would only forfeit their own reputation, as serious and practical men, by claiming it. Neither the past history of their Church, nor the instincts of her members at the present day, would afford any countenance to such unwise assumptions. The language of the Dean of Bristol interpreted fairly the mind both of her clergy and people, and harmonised with all the facts of her career. One of the most eminent of her living prelates had well observed, and he thought most of their colleagues would concur with his grace, that, as regards religion in general, and the sacred ministry in particular, "the Church of England was *meant to be* a compromise," which was surely only another way of stating the proposition of Dr. Elliot, that she was in all respects purely human.

ARCHDEACON JOLLY exclaimed abruptly: Not a "compromise," but a "comprehension." The latter was an emendation of the Bishop of Oxford. The difference, he apprehended, between the two was this; that whereas the Archbishop regarded the English Church as a *suppression* of the distinctions between truth and error, the Bishop of Oxford defended her as a *combination* of both, which showed that his lordship exactly agreed with the Dean of Bristol.

ARCHDEACON THEORY thought they were losing sight of the Apostolic Succession, and wished to revert to it. Without desiring to import into the debate an improper levity, he would ask: "Was it possible that the Apostolic Succession might be derived to the English Church through the *female* line?" (Great laughter.) At all events, their Church had accepted female pontiffs and adopted, with perfect docility, their spiritual edicts. Did not Elizabeth "dispense" all her clergy from what she herself called the "imperfections" of their Orders, and did not the clergy humbly accept the "dispensation?" If the first Fathers of the English Church publicly taught that the sovereign could make a bishop or priest "without ordination," Elizabeth might fairly take them at their word; and, as her authority alone made their "defective" Orders valid, was he not justified in saying that the succession had been preserved in the Church of England through the female line?

DR. EASY, with deference to the Archdeacon, would deprecate any discussion of that point. It was, indeed, certain that many of the most illustrious Reformers openly taught, with the evident approval of their contemporaries, that the election of their civil magistrate sufficed to constitute the ministerial office. But the Church of England, moulded into a peculiar form by the Tudors, accepted from them a semblance of the ancient sacerdotal hierarchy, keeping the names, but rejecting the realities which they represented. This was a part of the "compromise" to which the Archbishop had alluded. The acts of the great daughter of Henry VIII, alluded to by the Archdeacon, could only be understood by bearing in mind that, politically a Protestant, she was always in her secret heart a Roman Catholic. There was probably nothing on earth which she despised with such fierce contempt as her own bishops and clergy. "I made you a bishop, and by—— I will unfrock you," was the sort of language in which she addressed the unfortunate prelates who trembled before her. How she addressed their wives, and especially Mrs. Parker, he need not remind them. It had been suggested that two Roman augurs could not possibly have looked each other in the face without laughing; but he should like to know with what feelings two Elizabethan bishops, meeting in a safe place, where there were no witnesses to betray them, revealed their appreciation of one another.

It was useless to attempt to disguise the truth, in reviewing this humiliating part of their ecclesiastical history. Elizabeth was in a false position, and her keen sense of this fact only increased her exasperation. She used her new clergy as tools, giving them for political purposes titles and dignities which her conscience contemptuously refused them. If the Pope would have condoned the scandal of her birth, she would have lived and died a Catholic. But she was resolved to wear a crown; and as she could not reign with the Pope's consent, she determined to reign without it. Here was the clue to her whole history. It was a bitter humiliation to this proud woman, in whom all the arrogance of the Tudors was concentrated, to be obliged to ask the Catholic bishops of her realm,—whom she confessed to be true ones,—to have the goodness to consecrate her own, whom she despised in her inmost heart as time-serving impostors. But it was a still greater humiliation to be refused! She was too sagacious to tolerate the silly delusion, which had become popular in their own day, of "Anglo-Catholic" branch-Christianity. She knew what Catholic meant, and what Protestant meant, but had formed no conception of a hybrid monster begotten of the two. And, therefore, as she was not a woman to be content with half measures, she took up the axe of the executioner, and watered the new plant of her own supremacy with the blood of all who dared to question it. Her father had murdered Fisher, because that honest prelate refused to worship the idol which *he* had set up; and now the unfortunate Catholic clergy were carried in troops to Tyburn, because they declined to accept *her* as their Pope. But though her policy drove her to these deeds of blood, she seemed to soothe her conscience by manifesting her contempt for the new order of clergy, who humbly accepted all her decrees, and only asked what they were expected to believe and obey, in order to believe and obey with obsequious silence. Like the Russian Peter, who told his equally subservient bishops: "Since you will not have the Pope for your patriarch, you shall obey me only," Elizabeth treated the clergy of her own creation with a kind of ferocious disdain. The Catholics baffled her by dying. For their Protestant successors she reserved a worse fate, by allowing them to live. Over *them* she ruled as Pontiff with a cynical and remorseless tyranny at which their own age could afford to smile, but which was no laughing matter to their ancestors. It was difficult for an English clergyman of the nineteenth century, living under the mild sway of Queen Victoria, to comprehend how Elizabeth's bishops could tolerate their lot. It was, in truth, a gloomy hour. But good often came out of evil, and it was surely creditable to one of the most excellent of human institutions,—and he cared to claim no higher title for the Church of England,—that her respected clergy, though still dutifully subject to the civil magistrate, were no longer the slaves of his caprice; and that, in their own day, the successor of Parker was received as a gentleman and a guest by the successor of Elizabeth, without the fear of insult and mockery either for himself or his wife. (Loud applause.)

DEAN PRIMITIVE must utterly decline, for his own part, to see anything consoling in the fact which appeared to give so much pleasure to his reverend colleagues. The improved social condition of the English clergy,—which he would take leave to say was due mainly to their own merits,—might, indeed, be a subject for thankfulness; but he protested against the Erastian notion that it was a full compensation for the loss, which so many of his reverend friends seemed to accept with complete indifference, of every claim to anything higher than a purely earthly character.

DEAN BLUNT desired to recall the assembly from these collateral topics to the question of Anglican Orders, upon which, he presumed to think, there was still a good deal to be said. If they had any validity, in the sense of that term employed by the High-Church party, it could only be by reason of their derivation from Rome. Now here, as the learned Professor had justly intimated, they had to deal with two distinct lines of thought, one purely historical, the other belonging to the sphere of morals and theology. As to the first, which was the least important, he thought that no adequate proof had ever been given, or could be given, of the integrity of their Succession. The evidence which centuries had failed to complete would never be completed at all. It was surely a fatal note against their High-Church friends, that they had always been occupied in *vindicating* their Orders! The attitude of the rest of Christendom towards them sufficiently exposed their want of success.

A valued friend of his own, and a great ornament of the Puseyite party, had assured him, with a sorrowful gravity which he was incapable of treating with ridicule, that "for years he had been in the habit of asking God to forgive him, every time he stood before the altar, if he were not really a Catholic priest." He had reason to believe that, at least among the more earnest and conscientious members of that party, this was a common case.

But if the purely historical aspect of the question was, to put it at the lowest, a maze of doubt and peradventure, the moral difficulties were still more formidable, and darkened the whole ground with their portentous shadow. He would ask Archdeacon Chasuble, if he were not absorbed in conversation with his neighbour, to favour him with his attention, while he endeavoured to examine one only of these difficulties, of which the number was legion. Had the Archdeacon, and the clergy who shared his opinions, while consoling themselves with the belief that they derived their orders from Rome, ever seriously considered how such a claim could be reconciled with the language of the Reformers, including the principal founders and doctors of their own Church? The latter thought, and said, with an energy of expression which made all doubt about their meaning impossible, that for nearly a thousand years the whole Roman priesthood lay wallowing in idolatry and corruption. They proclaimed, as the all-sufficient defense of their own separation, that it was necessary to the salvation of every Christian soul to flee from that apostate Church, and to form a new religion, with Thirty-Nine new Articles of Christian belief, new forms of Christian worship, and new and frightful penalties for non-confirmity. For more than two hundred years, the English bishops, whom they were now bid to regard as *Catholics*, gave their hearty assent to laws which made it *death* to be reconciled to the Church of Rome, *death* to say or hear Mass, *death* to be, or to harbour, a priest; and, as if this were not a sufficient proof of their hatred to Rome, life-long imprisonment and confiscation of goods was the penalty either for sending a child to a Catholic country for education, or having him brought up a Catholic at home.

But this was not all. During that whole period, and from the first hour of her existence, all the pulpits of the National Church had resounded with imprecations against the Roman sorceress, and successive generations of Englishmen were carefully nurtured *by the bishops and clergy*, in that passionate abhorrence of the very name of Catholic which distinguished them to this day. Their very literature had been formed in the same spirit, which breathed in every page, not only of episcopal charges and parochial sermons, but even of biographies and works of fiction, the same unflagging hatred of the religion which England had abolished.

And now, in spite of these well-known facts, they were seriously told, that during all this time they had been Catholics without knowing it; their bishops heirs of St. Augustine, St. Anselm, and St. Thomas of Canterbury; and their ministers sacrificing priests, full of reverence for the mysteries of the altar, and the august sacrament of penance! He wished to speak calmly, but he would venture to ask: Was ever God so mocked? (Sensation.)

He was persuaded that no one in that assembly would venture to deny, that *all* the English reformers, the very men who founded their Church and gave them their formularies, had branded the Catholic Church with more prodigious curses than the Saviour of men had ever predicted for her blessings and triumphs. And yet they were now to be told that all this was a mistake,—a mere display of harmless rhetoric; and that, as a matter of fact, the English clergy were identical, in office and in gifts, with their Roman brethren! He could understand that any one who objected to the language of the Reformers, and had learned to abhor their doctrines, should humbly sue for pardon and reconciliation with the Holy See; but that a community which had such an origin, and such a history, as their own, should pretend to be anxious about its unbroken connection with Rome, and claim to be in all essentials one with her, and to have common orders and common sacraments, and to form part of the great Christian commonwealth, precisely because it could boast filial generation from *her;* there was in this notion such an audacious denial of truth and common sense,—considering what the Church of England had ever been, and still was,—that it was difficult to treat it seriously. That an Anglican minister, a disciple of the Articles and the Homilies, a successor of Cranmer and Jewel, of Abbot and Whitgift,—holding perhaps a benefice once held by a Catholic priest, and ministering at a table which had been substituted for a Catholic altar,—should venture to say all this; besides being the most intolerable insult to his own Church, was as if a man should contend proudly for a pedigree derived through countless generations of felons. What! call the whole

Catholic priesthood "the spawn of Antichrist," as your own fathers did, and then attempt to prove that your Orders are manifestly divine, because you can trace them to *that* source; revile the whole Catholic Church as "the harlot of Babylon," as twenty generations of your own bishops and clergy did, and then claim her as your Mother! Surely this was either the last and wildest eccentricity of the human mind, or else the most impudent trifling with serious things of which any age or country could furnish an example.

ARCHDEACON CHASUBLE was content to reply to the Dean that the whole scaffolding of his discourse tumbled to pieces before the simple fact, that many English clergymen, of whom he was proud to be one, utterly denied that the Roman Church had ever been anti-Christian, or her clergy apostate.

DEAN BLUNT would, in that case, suggest to the Archdeacon to transfer his reproaches and anathemas from the Church which, in his opinion, had never deserved them, to the impious community which had dared to utter them. (Loud cheers.) It was, of course, open to Archdeacon Chasuble and his friends to repudiate the language of the men who composed the Articles and Homilies; but let them repudiate at the same time the work which they did and the Church which they founded. No man, they were told, could serve two masters. Let the Archdeacon beware lest he fall between two stools. No proposition, he conceived, could be more indisputable than this,—that if the Church of Rome did not deserve the curses which the Church of England had heaped upon her, they must recoil upon the latter. If the Church of Rome was their mother, their sister, or in any other degree related to them; if she was the source of their Order, and therefore of their sacraments, and therefore of their highest spiritual blessings, according to the doctrine of High-Churchmen; then were the founders of the Church of England, and nearly all her members up to the present hour, monsters of ingratitude, calumny, and falsehood. It was as impossible to profess esteem for both Churches at once, as it would be to serve God and Satan at the same moment, and by the same act. Men must choose between the two, and except the consequences of their choice. One thing alone they could *not* do, they could not, with the Reformers, separate from the Catholic Church on the ground that she was "Anti-Christian," and yet assert, with the Puseyites, that they were themselves the legitimate descendants of Antichrist. (General marks of approval.)

ARCHDEACON CHASUBLE had never denied, and would not begin by denying now, the painful and distressing difficulties which beset clergymen of his own views in dealing with these momentous subjects. But where doubt and uncertainty seemed to be their providential lot, he must consider it the mark of a Christian temper to accept such crosses in a humble and patient spirit. He was not disposed to cut the Gordian knot of their difficulties, but would rather continue to bear than seek escape from them by so rude a process. If, however, he could not, as he freely admitted, refuse a certain measure of assent to the arguments of the Dean, nor dispute that a vast majority of English Churchmen had always accepted the principles and maxims upon which they were founded, he would at least venture to reply to them by a *reductio ad absurdum*, and ask their advocates if *they* were prepared to accept all the conclusions which logically flowed from them.

It was, every one would admit, a necessary result of the Dean's reasoning that Dr. Arnold was quite right when he said, that his butler had as much divine authority to administer the sacraments as himself. Where all were laymen, and the possession of merely *human* Orders left them all in that condition, all were equally qualified, as respected supernatural powers, to handle the mysteries of religion. The Tower of Babel, on this hypothesis, was the only true type of the Christian Church and ministry. For his part, he must object to an ecclesiastical economy which would admit of his butler or his tailor proposing to ordain him priest or bishop, on the ground that *their* succession from the Apostles and that of the Bishop of London were equally susceptible, or equally destitute, of proof. He respected Authority. (Cries of "Oh! oh!") He was speaking for himself, and repeated that he respected Authority, and venerated Order. He could not believe that of all the works of God the Church must be the least symmetrical and harmonious, the most confused and disorderly; and therefore he demanded some higher credential of divine commission than a man's own appreciation of his personal fitness. He could not detect the signs of an

Apostle in one who elected himself, or was elected by his congregation, on the ground that his ideas of Christianity and their own were sufficiently alike. It everybody was equally qualified to teach religion, it was manifest that nobody required to be taught. He should like to accompany the Professor to certain churches which he would not name, but of which the incumbents shared the opinions of the Dean of Bristol and Dr. Arnold. He would suppose the clergyman to choose for his text, "*Rebuke with all authority,*" and would ask if he might not be reasonably expected to deliver some such discourse as the following: "My brethren, as I have no more right to rebuke you than you have to rebuke me, and only just so much authority to teach as you are willing to confer upon me, permit me to observe to you, Now to God the Father," &c. (Great laughter.) The Dean would not deny that such a sermon would aptly express the preacher's conviction, that Anglican Orders were purely human. Again, he would suppose such a clergyman to preach from the words, "*Watch over the flock of which the Holy Ghost has made you overseer, in order to govern the Church of God.*" Evidently, if he would do justice to his own belief, he ought to address his flock in such terms as the following: "As it is you who are watching over me, and not I over you, and as my sole function is to tickle your itching ears, you will kindly pardon me if I make the unpleasant ceremony as brief as possible, and quit the pulpit at once. This will save me from occupying a ridiculous position, and spare you the trouble of criticising a sermon which it is not my intention to deliver. Clerk, give out a hymn, and make your own choice." Once more, he would ask if it did not result from the Professor's view of the character of the English Church, which Dr. Elliot called "the creature of the law," and which a living archbishop declared was "meant to be a compromise," that when our Lord said, "*Go, and teach all nations,*" He signified the command, "Go, and let all nations teach *you.*" So, also, when St. Paul affirmed, "*No man taketh to himself this honour but he that is called of God, as was Aaron,*" he doubtless wished the Corinthians to understand, "Every man *ought* to take this honour to himself if he aspire to it, for the age of Aaron is excessively remote, and his example perfectly obsolete." In like manner, when the same Apostle said, "*How shall they preach, except they be sent?*" many of the clergy would aptly reply, "As to preaching, I find no difficulty in it; and as to being sent, I send myself."

He thought he had sufficiently indicated what must be the inevitable result of the Dean's principles in the spiritual, and he would now beg him to consider what kind of fruits they would produce in the social order. Young gentlemen would evidently present *themselves* to commissions in the army. Policemen would display their robust forms, without the sanction of Sir Richard Mayne, wherever they deemed it advantageous to the interests of the public, or their own. Students of various degrees of maturity would call themselves to the bar, or take their seats in Parliament, or even in the Cabinet, amply commissioned by the rational conviction that Cicero and Demosthenes were but their imperfect types, and only designed by nature to prepare the way for their incomparable successors. Finally, persons addicted to an immoral preference for the goods of others, or disposed to indulge in a premature repetition of the marriage rites, would enjoy the privilege of taking themselves up as their own policemen, trying themselves as their own jury, and acquitting themselves as their own judge. And the eccentricities of these various classes, he would venture to add, would be both less grotesque and less hurtful to society than the pranks of a national clergy, distinguished only by the colour of a cravat from the laymen around them, and presuming to handle divine things with only a human vocation.

He would earnestly entreat that due consideration be given to the fact that, on the principle laid down by the Dean, all the English clergy, excepting only those who candidly repudiated all pretence to a supernatural calling, were simply criminal and dangerous impostors. He would go further, and say, without fear of contradiction, that if English Orders were *human*, he could conceive nothing in creation so degraded, nothing so worthy of a nation's mockery and scorn, as an Anglican bishop. On that supposition, their prelates were an offence against truth, and a scandal in the land. For his part, he would rather be a strolling pieman, or an acrobat at a fair. Such men as these might possibly deserve esteem, because they followed a calling for which they had the necessary gifts; but an unconsecrated bishop should be scourged from the face of the earth. He was a thing to make the angels weep. His whole life was a lie. He was to be utterly abhorred and execrated, and should be received everywhere, as Dr. Alexander was on his entrance into Jerusalem, with a shower of mud and stones.

Ah! he had never expected to hear it gravely discussed in such an assembly, whether English Orders were human or divine. His heart was oppressed with anguish in listening to such a debate. The Orders of the English Church he believed to be identical with those of the Roman, and, like them, divine in origin, in succession, and in power. If he could doubt it, he would flee from the National Church as from a pestilence; for it would be shame and death to minister at an altar which was only a table, and where every pseudo-priestly act was a grimace and a sham, a mockery of God, of one's neighbour, and of one's own soul.

(Some moments elapsed after the Archdeacon had ceased to speak before any one rose to claim the attention of the meeting. The clergy seemed to be occupied in whispering to one another their impressions of what they had just heard. Some observed that he had not attempted to answer Dean Blunt's arguments, and others that his retort was sophistical, because no one maintained that the clergy could take cures without the sanction of the civil magistrate. At length Dean Critical rose from an arm-chair by the side of the Professor of History, with whom he had been engaged in animated conversation, and advancing to the opposite corner of the chimney-piece, which Archdeacon Chasuble had just vacated, addressed himself to the assembly with a calm voice and subdued manner.)

It had never, he said, been his fortune on any previous occasion to hear a grave person deliver a solemn harangue from the top of a house of cards. Prudent builders secured their foundation before they put on the roof, but the Archdeacon began with his spire, and worked placidly downwards to the crypt. Long before he arrived at that lower region, his pack of cards had disappeared, and of his fancy edifice not a trace remained. He wanted the robust courage of the Archdeacon, and would crave permission to explain why he declined to inhabit the shadowy structure of so sentimental an architect.

He had asked himself several times during the speech of the Archdeacon, (he said it without any unkind or disrespectful feeling,) whether human reason and conscience, weak as the one might be and deceitful as was the other, could really accept,

without misgiving, the lot with which he avowed himself content.
What! *doubt* as to the heritage of Orders, with the sure possession
of which you deemed all spiritual treasures indissolubly bound up!—
doubt as to the validity of consecrations, which could never be
proved, and were morally and materially impossible, but upon the
efficacy of which your whole religious life hung!—*doubt* as to the
possession of Powers, your claim to which was as vehemently
derided by nine-tenths of your own community as by the whole
world without it, but the want of which reduced you to spiritual
atrophy and death!—*doubt* as to your generation from a Church,
in which you professed to find the cradle of your own, but against
which the latter was a living protest, and which in turn, far from
admitting the parentage, refused to regard you in any other light
than as heathens or heretics in need of conversion!—*doubt* both as
to her doctrines and your own, the first being rejected by you in
spite of the Roman Church bidding you to embrace them, and the
second maintained by you in spite of the English Church forbidding
you to hold them!—*doubt* as to your origin, *doubt* as to your
history, and *doubt* as to your future!—*doubt* as to doctrine, priesthood, and sacraments!—*doubt* as to whence you came, what you
are, and whither you are going! Ah! truly it was a marvel that
men like the Archdeacon could move under the burden of such a
creed, which could neither soothe the soul nor satisfy the intellect,
and which was as earnestly condemned by all outside their own
Church, as it was ridiculed by almost all within her.

How different was his own position, and that of the bishops and
clergy whose principles he shared! Disavowing all foolish claims
to supernatural powers, which were rebuked by their past history
as well as by their present habits of life and character, they accepted
the Reformation as a just attempt to reduce the Christian religion
to its true limits as a perfect system of morals, of which the sole
dogmatic basis was the doctrine of the Atonement. With this
profession of faith, they had a sufficient key to heaven, and needed
not the unreal arts of an obsolete priesthood, which warred against
the true genius of Christianity. To instruct the ignorant, to console
the afflicted, and to hold up to all the perfect work of the Saviour,
this was their religion, as he believed it was that of the apostles.
The claims of the Roman Church were nothing to them, for they
simply put them aside. They approved, on the whole, the censures

pronounced by the founders of Anglicanism, though they regretted the intemperance of the language which their peculiar position explained and partly excused. They had no difficulties and no doubts; and their creed, which reduced the mysteries of religion to those concerning the Person and office of the Son of God, and made but little account of sacraments, was as much in harmony with the wants of a healthy soul as with the conceptions of a sound mind. They were Protestant ministers, not Catholic priests; and if their religion separated them from the rest of the Christian world, it was surely better honestly to acknowledge a fact which they could not change, and which reflected no discredit upon them, than to affect to disguise it by transparent sophistry and paltry subterfuge. (General cheering.)

DEAN PRIMITIVE would venture to ask how his learned friend, who would not hear of mysteries nor of their priestly stewards and dispensers, disposed of the commission given by our Lord to His Apostles to bind and loose sins? or how he dealt with the awful texts setting forth the Real Presence?

DEAN CRITICAL was quite content to accept the rational interpretation which had always been put upon such passages by his own Church; and if there was any doubt or dispute about her teaching on such points, all who heard him would admit that at least there could be none whatever about her *practice*. But he would beg leave to continue his observations. Let them consider some of the practical consequences which ensued upon the claim of certain Protestant ministers to possess and use the powers of Catholic priests. It seemed to him that if he held the opinions of his High-Church brethren, his first thought would be to conceal them from all mankind in the secret of his own heart. He should not dare to avow, because he should not dare to act upon them. How, for example, could he venture, without the slightest preparation from childhood upwards, born of the world and belonging to it in all his interests, feelings, and habits, to make pretence of hearing confessions without the sanction of his superiors, or to offer a semblance of Mass in disloyal opposition to it? How could he teach with a grave face that sacramental absolution was the ordinary instrument for the remission of sin, when he knew that his own Church had utterly neglected to employ this mighty instrument during three centuries, (which she could hardly have done if she had been conscious of possessing it,) and that he himself was quite ready to give communion to people who never had received, and never intended to ask for, such absolution? How could he mock himself and his hearers by teaching that the Protestant Reformation, of which the main object was to uproot the Catholic religion with all its distinctive tenets and practices, was really designed to preserve it intact in this realm? How could he remain voluntarily, year after year, in close ecclesiastical communion with bishops and clergy who execrated doctrines which *he* held to be divine, and spent their lives in teaching their contraries? How could he say to the world without a blush, "I attach so little importance to the mysterious doctrines which I profess with my lips, that, as you see, I continue to give my allegiance to a bishop who condemns them, and remain in fraternal bonds with a clergy which blasphemes them?" God keep them all from such dishonour as this, the worst and most grievous reproach which could rest on the conscience of a Christian man. Better far to be ignorant of the most precious doctrines of the Christian covenant, than to trample under foot, by such revolting insincerity, the very truths which they professed to honour. (Loud applause.)

And now let him refer, in conclusion, to that peculiar mystery which surpassed all others in the effects which it had produced in modifying the form and character of Christian worship in all save Protestant communities. He alluded to the mystery which might be said to constitute the main spring of religious life in all the Eastern and Western Churches alike, except only their own. In the Catholic and Oriental Churches, its seat was the altar, and its home was the tabernacle. A lamp burned night and day before it; and from early morn to the hour which called all to rest, silent worshippers adored the majesty of that mystical Presence in which they had been taught from childhood to believe, and which was not more securely guarded from what they would deem profanation by a minute and elaborate ritual, than by the tender instinct and jealous devotion of the faithful themselves.

Now, Archdeacon Chasuble and his friends professed to have the power to consecrate the Host. He would ask leave to address to them a serious question. Would they maintain, in the face of history and of the unanimous testimony of the whole people of these islands, that any provision whatever was made for such a guest in the Church of England? Where was the tabernacle? broken into fragments like the altar upon which it once stood! Where was the ritual, defining with more than legal precision how such a mystery should be handled? It was utterly silent on the whole subject, declaring only that Christ's body could not be "in two places at once," leaving the poor shadow to the caprice of minister and people, and sternly forbidding that the reality should be "lifted up or worshipped." Did this look like a design on the part of the English Church to furnish a lodging for what the Catholics called "the sacramental king?" It would be a sentence of death upon her to suppose it. Either she believed the mystery, and did not care to make *any preparation for it*, which would be charging her with irreverence, such as fiends could not surpass, or she utterly rejected it, and then her ritual and her practice enforced and illustrated the denial.

If his High-Church friends,—who really seemed to him to believe nothing so little as the very dogmas which they professed to regard with solemn awe, but of which they tranquilly contemplated the utter desecration day by day in their own communion,—would consider what had been the attendant circumstances, already glanced at by previous speakers, in every celebration of the Lord's Supper during three hundred years, he conceived that they would not dare to impute to the Church of England any belief in the Real Presence. It would be a gratuitous outrage upon her. Using always common leavened bread,—as if on purpose to multiply the chances of accident, against which she literally made no provision whatever, so utterly indifferent was she to the whole matter,—crumbs must inevitably be scattered about the communion rails, and be abandoned to whatever fate might befall them, including that of being removed by an old woman with her shovel on the Monday morning. Moreover, whole masses of "consecrated" bread and wine, not consumed by the communicants, were afterwards, in a multitude of parishes, and even in some of their cathedrals, left to the discretion of the clerk, who took them home, or cast them into a graveyard, or otherwise disposed of these despised fragments of a divine banquet, at his own caprice. And their Prayer-Book contained nothing to prevent such acts, to which bishops and other dignitaries were constantly consenting parties. Now he had taken pains to inquire of a Roman Catholic friend what was the practice of his Church? Her rubrics, which he had examined, seemed to make provision for every conceivable accident which could possibly occur, and minutely directed in what manner they should severally be dealt with. If, in spite of every precaution, a particle should fall to the ground,—an event, he was assured, which was almost unknown,—it was immediately raised with all reverence and replaced in the Paten or Ciborium, and at the close of the service the clergy went in procession, and, kneeling on their knees, cut out the piece of the carpet on which the particle had fallen, and carefully consumed it by fire. Well these men were at least consistent. God forbid that he should sneer at them. They practised what they professed to believe, and what, doubtless, they did believe. But how was it, how had it ever been, in the English Church? Suppose there were in England ten thousand churches, and that the Lord's Supper had been celebrated in each of them four times a year for three hundred years. It would follow, on the theory of High-Churchmen, that a stupendous sacrilege had been enacted in England, since the Reformation, at least twelve million times; and that the worst horrors and ignominies of the Passion had been renewed in the Church of England, without fear and without remorse, every time communion was given to her members. For his part, he would abandon that Church on the instant in horror and trembling, if he held the opinions of Archdeacon Chasuble. But he hastened to add, that there was nothing in what he had said to disturb the most timid conscience. The appalling scenes which he had imagined had never really occurred. The Church of England believed nothing of these dread mysteries, and *therefore* made no provision against their profanation. He would take the liberty to add, that it was very evident his High-Church friends did not believe them either; for if they did, they could not remain another hour in the English Church.

(At this moment the door was thrown open, and a solemn butler, who might easily have been mistaken for a bishop in plain clothes, announced, as if he were giving out a refreshing text, that "tea was served." The company descended to the dining-room, where they found an entertainment worthy of their host and of themselves.

Mr. Kidds volunteered to say grace, but, becoming tedious, was pulled back into his chair by his nearest neighbour. Dean Blunt and Archdeacon Chasuble found themselves side by side, and entered into cheerful conversation, neither seeming to remember their recent conflict, nor to have the least intention to "abandon the Church," a phrase which apparently had no particular meaning, but was kept ready for use whenever the occasion required it. Archdeacon Jolly inquired across the table of Mr. Kidds, who was eating a muffin, whether he had seen a pamphlet, published by —— & Co., and entitled, "Hints on the Easier Methods of Leading Captive Silly Women: By one who has had Experience in the Ministry." Mr. Kidds replied, with some asperity, that he knew nothing whatever, and desired to know nothing, of such a book; but he had seen an advertisement of one called, "Suggestions for a New Religion," and had imagined that it might perhaps be a production of Archdeacon Jolly. Dr. Critical asked Dean Primitive if he had seen Dr. Pusey's recent observations in the *Guardian* about the probable advent of "a Free Church," and as the Dean only shook his head, proceeded to observe, that it was an equivocal commentary on his supposed belief in the perpetuity of the Establishment, and showed what a very clear idea he entertained of the nature of a Teaching Church. Evidently Dr. Pusey thought that it was lawful to create a new one any day of the week. Dean Pliable said that he had in his pocket a tract which was likely to assist Dr. Pusey's "free church," and could only be the production of some very indiscreet disciple of that eminent divine. Its title was this: "Is Baptism Necessary for a Christian Bishop?" It seemed intended to prove that, owing to the "careless administration of the rite" in past times, a large proportion of Anglican Bishops had probably been unbaptized. It was a very reckless and imprudent pamphlet, and yet he could not deny that it contained some serious and even startling suggestions. He would read a passage or two from it while his friends drank their tea.

"Recall for a moment the spectacle of a public baptism in many of our large parish churches, so late as even twenty years ago. A crowd of infants, shrouded in caps and enveloped in flannels, were held in the arms of their nurses round a font which had nothing in it but a small basin of water. The clergyman, standing on the *other* side of the font, spirted a few drops of the fluid from the tip of one finger at each baby in turn, or rather at the heap of clothes under which it was hidden. It was a hundred to one that the rite was not administered in a single case, and a thousand to one that it was not administered in all. Moreover, it was almost certain that there was no sufficient connection between the sacramental words and the pouring of the water, even supposing that the water had really flowed on the head of a single child. Whole generations of clergymen in the English Church,—Puritans, Evangelicals, or worldlings,—all nearly equally indifferent about the administration of a sacrament to which they attached very little importance, had unconsciously conspired together to breed an unbaptized population in these islands. The fact is simply appalling in its effect upon our ecclesiastical *status*. An unbaptized man could neither receive nor confer ordination."

Dean Pompous entreated that they might hear no more of a tract so pestilent and revolutionary; but Dean Primitive observed that, only thirteen years ago, it had happened to himself to witness an utterly invalid baptism in one of the churches in Hampshire, and that he had great difficulty in obtaining the repetition of the ineffectual ceremony. Dr. Easy also remarked that his predecessor in the living which he held in the country *always* baptized the children with what he himself called "a damp finger;" and he had heard of a large church in a manufacturing town where, during a whole winter, water was never used at all, because, as the Vicar observed in explanation, "it was too cold for the babies." Here the clergy began to leave their chairs, as if they found the subject distasteful, and ascended to the drawing-room. Dean Primitive and Archdeacon Chasuble alone remained, apparently with design. "Chasuble," said his friend, "I am sick at heart. What answer can be made to Blunt and the Professor? If our Orders are a delusion, what are *we?*" "Alas! my friend," replied the Archdeacon, "I begin to suspect that the validity of our Orders is a much less important question than we had supposed. There are other doubts which affect me more painfully." Silence ensued for several minutes, when the Archdeacon, rising with a deep sigh from his chair, said: "Primitive, let us go up stairs."

The clergy had resumed their seats, awaiting the renewal of the debate, when the Rev. Athanasius Benedict, a young man of pleasant aspect, but wearing the robe of a monk, advanced into the room with quick step and eager manner. Apologising to Dr. Easy for the lateness of his arrival, he explained that he had only that evening reached London from Rome, whither he had been to consult the most famous theologians on several points of great interest. (Some of the clergy laughed, and Mr. Kidds exclaimed, "truly disgusting.") He had seen the Pope for a few moments, and received his blessing; but his Holiness declined to admit him to a second interview, which he very much regretted, as he was anxious to convince him of the catholicity of the English Church. However, he had seen Cardinal Barnabo at his official residence, who received him courteously, and seemed disposed to listen to his questions; but unfortunately an oriental bishop happened to come in on business, and his Eminence requested him to call another day. He had intended to ask him whether there was any Catholic precedent by which an individual might appoint *himself* superior of a religious order of his own creation, without having made any previous noviciate; whether, if his bishop was an ignorant heretic, he might treat his foolish opposition with contempt; whether, in case of necessity, he might teach his Church, supposing his Church to be incapable of teaching him; whether, if he should be excommunicated by all his monks, and excommunicate them all in return, it was his duty or theirs to pay the debts of the monastery; whether—(Dr. Easy here observed somewhat stiffly, that the subject under consideration at that meeting, was the character of English Orders, and though it had perhaps been sufficiently discussed, if the reverend gentleman desired to make any remarks, he presumed the assembly would hear him. He trusted, however, that he would endeavour to be brief. Without a moment's hesitation, and looking straight before him with a piercing glance, the Rev. Athanasius Benedict spoke as follows:)

He had sometimes been tempted to doubt the integrity of English Orders, but he had put away the sinful thought as a snare of the enemy. It was his rule not to listen to any suggestions tending to disparage the Anglo-Catholic Church. He would admit, however, that if Christendom refused to recognise the English clergy as priests, there was some excuse for the error. The clergy themselves were responsible for it. As long as they were incessantly "marry-ing and giving in marriage," so as to be known to the world chiefly as types of uxorious effeminacy, their priesthood would be rejected as a fable. The world had not been converted by married priests, and never would be. Their example would always do more to encourage worldliness than their teaching to restrain vice. But if it shocked the purest instincts of the soul to see a priest entangled in wedlock, what language could do justice to the revolting spectacle of a wedded bishop? The primitive Christians, he was persuaded, would have recoiled with horror from such an object. (Dean Pompous, crimson with indignation, protested that he would leave the room if the young man repeated such disgraceful language.) Oh! he was aware that such views were out of harmony with the actual spirit of the English Church, but it was necessary to reform that spirit, and by God's help they would do it. A Gregory VII. would be raised up in their communion, to purify the defiled courts of the temple. St. Paul, who was a greater authority than the Church of England, had delivered his testimony against a married clergy. "It is good for man," he said, speaking even of the laity, "*not* to touch a woman." And the Master whom St. Paul served, had taught that there was a special choir in heaven, clothed with its own peculiar glory, and composed of those only "who had not defiled themselves with women." What deadness of heart or bluntness of intellect could resist the arguments of the Apostle: "He that is with a wife is solicitous for the things of the world, how he may please his wife!" Why should they receive this divine admonition as if it were addressed to others, but had no application to themselves? What had they gained by despising it? What better illustration could the world give of its truth, or of the shameful incongruity of a married priesthood, than that latest invention of connubial repose, an English parsonage-house, or that triumphant device of luxurious ease, an English Episcopal palace? (Here Dean Pompous abruptly left the room. Some of the clergy inquired in whispers whether Mr. Benedict should be allowed to continue. It seemed to be agreed that he should, and he did.)

It was only, he said, (watching with a smile the retreating figure of Dean Pompous,) by taking to pieces the idea of a married priesthood, and viewing it in its detached phenomena, that one could hope to realise its grotesque character. He would say nothing of it as a confession of feeble and maudlin worldliness, nor of its glaring inconsistency with all that was great, and noble, and fruitful, in

Christian annals. It did not deserve to be treated so seriously. But he would come to familiar details. For example; a sacerdotal wedding-tour was a thing which struck the fancy as unique. To appreciate such an expedition fully, they must consider it as the last of a long series of preliminary incidents, all belonging to what was sometimes playfully called the "spoony" type. During this period, the enamoured pastor might be contemplated as alternating between thrilling sermons on "taking up the cross," and rapturous interviews with the lady of his love. One moment he might be seen at the altar, and the next in the boudoir; now discriminating the claims of two equally fascinating doctrines, and a little later adjusting the merits of two equally adorable bonnets. But he would not pursue the subject in its various details. He would only observe, that perhaps the most ardent admirer of hymeneal rites would cheerfully admit, that he could not conceive St. Paul or St. John starting on a nuptial tour, accompanied by the "latest fashions" from Athens or Ephesus, and the graceful brides whom they were destined to adorn. They would feel that Christianity itself could not survive such a vision as that. Nor could the imagination picture, in its wildest mood, the majestic adversary of the Arian emperor attended on his flight up the Nile by Mistress Athanasius; nor St. John Chrysostom escorted in his wanderings through Phrygia by the wife of his bosom, arrayed in a wreath of orange blossoms. Would Ethelbert have become a Christian, if St. Augustine had introduced to him his lady and her bridesmaids? No, the instincts of man could not tolerate the Apostolical Succession taking its recreation in a honeymoon.

For his own part, moved by the thought of what the great preachers of the gospel had ever been, in every age, he was accustomed to say to himself, whenever he met a clergyman with a woman under his arm: "There is a gentleman who would certainly not have consented to be ordained, if he had thought there was the faintest risk of his losing by the transaction." He knew it was sometimes said,—for men were ingenious in apologising for their infirmities, and especially for those to which they were most inclined —that such priests might be models to their flocks of domestic virtue. Would that they were always even that! But the world expected priests to be models of something higher. There were plenty of people to serve as models of domestic virtue. He gladly admitted that there were in the English Church worthy husbands and fathers of families; but where were the successors of the Baptist, of St. Stephen, or St. James? Alas! not in their own communion, though they abounded elsewhere. Only the other day, as he came through France, he read in a French journal the martyrdom of nine French bishops and priests at once in Corea. Did any one suppose that if they had been married, they would have coveted the crown of martyrdom? "He that is married," said the apostle, "is solicitous for *the things of the world;*" and for that reason there were no Anglican missionaries in Corea. There never would be any, unless it happened to become quite safe to go there. *Eleven* Colonial bishops, they learned from the *Times*, were in England about a year ago, having left their distant sees to take care of themselves; a new proof of the soft and luxurious temper which marriage fostered in the clergy.

It would be impossible to enumerate all the evils which flowed from this source. It was hardly too much to say that in their own day, as in past times, the imposition of hands by an English bishop was simply an indication of his opinion that the candidate before him had an undoubted vocation for matrimony. It was sad to be obliged to confess that it had been so in their Church from the beginning. As Erasmus said, marriage was the only paradise left to a "reformed" Christian. In the theology of the founders of Anglicanism, Nuptials and Orders were equivalent terms; but the last was only valued as an introduction to the first. He remembered a fact in the life of Bishop Barlow, a name of evil omen for them, which fitly inaugurated the religious revolution of the sixteenth century. Five of that prelate's daughters married five Anglican bishops,—no doubt with the pious intention of keeping alive the Apostolical Succession in the Church of England.

And it was to be observed that when a clergyman once married, it seemed impossible to revive in him any respect for continence. He would marry every year, if his wives would only die fast enough to allow him to do so. St. Paul had said, speaking of a society which had just been formed out of the ranks of the heathen: "a bishop should be the husband of *one* wife." He could not possibly mean that all bishops must be married men, since he earnestly dissuaded even the devout laity from excepting the yoke of marriage. He evidently implied by these words, that any one who had been married twice, even as a heathen layman, was utterly unworthy to become a Christian bishop. Yet some of their own most creditable bishops, men who had left a name behind them, had actually married twice *after* they had been raised to the episcopate. The late Bishop of Salisbury did so, and defended the shameful deed in a charge to his clergy! He took this to be the most stupendous fact in ecclesiastical story.

They were perhaps aware that even in Russia, a semi-barbarous country, where a married priesthood was permitted, and where the law had hitherto compelled every son of a priest to become a priest himself, because nobody else would accept the office, he was absolutely prohibited from marrying *after* he was ordained. That was too much even for Russian insensibility. But he perceived that some of the company were becoming impatient, and would detain them no longer. He had come there to deliver his testimony, and it was a relief to his conscience to have done so. He had not heard the previous debate on their Orders, but perhaps there was no more formidable argument against them than one which had often been addressed to himself during his travels. "If your clergy were true priests," he had been told, "they would display the supernatural virtues which accompany a divine vocation. But they are simply fathers of families, like any other laymen. The grace of Orders does not appear in them, therefore they are not validly ordained." He believed he was not deficient in courage, but he never heard this argument without trying to change the conversation. It was not, however, in his nature weakly to despair. The day would come, and he fondly believed that it was at hand, when the reproach of a married clergy would be taken away from them. The first Anglican Council, to which all hearts were now looking forward, would prohibit sacerdotal nuptials. When that auspicious day arrived, he should no longer blush to meet his Roman and Russian friends, for he should be able to tell them that he had judged the Holy Anglican Church more wisely than they, and had not erred in predicting the glorious resurrection reserved for her, and the triumphant demonstration of the validity of her Orders.

(For some moments no one seemed inclined to reply to Mr. Benedict, who was evidently regarded by the company as a very obnoxious person. At length Mr. Kidds arose, and shaking himself free from the grasp of two neighbours, who tried forcibly to hold him down, spoke thus :)

He presumed that Mr. Benedict was a Roman priest in disguise. (Mr. Benedict smiled.) But he would meet him face to face, and confound him with the sword of the Spirit. He wished to deprive the clergy of the evangelical solaces of domestic life, and quoted Paul in defence of his unholy project. For his part, he doubted not that Paul, who was a spiritual man, corrected his error on the subject of matrimony, which might be attributed to his Jewish education, or, perhaps, to the fact that he was by natural disposition averse to the female sex. In his judgment, there was not to be seen on this planet an object so melancholy and repugnant as a Roman priest. He never met one without feeling—well, he could hardly express what he felt ——

MR. BENEDICT would ask permission to express it for him. He felt probably how deplorable must be the corruptions of that Church which preferred mortification to sensuality, the shadow of the Cross to the glare of the world, the example of St. Paul to that of Cranmer, and a life of devotion to sacerdotal duties to the sweet attractions of the drawing-room or the lofty delights of the nursery.

MR. KIDDS (who did not seem quite sure that that was exactly what he meant) replied, with a scornful wave of the hand, that he had been in Rome! He repeated (here he raised his voice to a very high pitch) that he had been in Rome, and there he had witnessed the pernicious effects of this unscriptural avoidance of matrimony. He had watched in the Corso and on the Pincio those odious Franciscans, degraded beings with naked feet and a rope round their waists, dirty and repulsive victims of a grovelling and humiliating superstition. That shocking spectacle had filled him with devout thankfulness for the blessed institutions of his own beloved Church and country, and had satisfied him that an unmarried clergy must necessarily be examples of crime and sources of corruption. He knew nothing more worthy of praise in the bishops of their Protestant community than the example which they gave in this matter. He rejoiced to believe that the unnatural spectacle of an unwedded bishop had never been seen, or very rarely, in their scriptural Church. Long might they continue to use their "Christian liberty," as the late Bishop Denison powerfully observed, and to adorn the land with a comely and godly offspring. This was the prayer of a truly Evangelical clergy, and he presumed that here at least the Puseyites were of one mind with them, since he knew that Dr. Primitive and Archdeacon Chasuble had both of them large families, and he believed that they both had daughters married to clergymen.

MR. BENEDICT, (whose face was illuminated with smiles,) trusted Mr. Kidds would bear with him while he said a word on behalf of those Roman monks whose dress and doctrines were equally distasteful to gentlemen of his views. He was not the advocate of Rome, and believed that it was the sublime destiny of the Anglican Church, in spite of present shortcomings, to restore both the Latin and Greek communion to the perfection which they had lost, and to admit both, after due instruction and correction, to the privilege of fellowship with herself. His poor prayers would never cease to be offered, that both the Eastern and Western Churches might be remodelled after the pattern of the English. But he could not admit that, because these less favoured churches had at present the misfortune to be separated from their own, therefore they contained nothing worthy to be esteemed or imitated. The Roman monks, with many of whom he was well acquainted, led a life of prayer, mortification, and good works. It was true they laboured under what an Englishman would consider disadvantages. They had not read Colenso on the "Pentateuch," nor the Oxford "Essays and Reviews," nor the discussions of Convocation of the two Provinces of York and Canterbury, nor even the sermons of Dr. Elliot, Dean of Bristol. They did not take in the *Times* or the *Saturday Review*. They had never heard of Dr. Lushington, nor of the Court of Arches; nor had they sat under Dr. Cumming, nor listened to the balmy eloquence of Samuel, Bishop of Oxford, and Lord High Almoner to the Queen. With all these disadvantages, it were unjust to expect that the Roman monks should know much of "modern enlightenment." Moreover, the branch of the great Franciscan family which was found in southern Italy and Sicily, was mainly recruited from the humbler orders. Like the fishermen of the Lake of Galilee, they were poor men ministering to the poor.

Their dress was sometimes ragged, but he supposed the wardrobe of the Apostles was also imperfectly furnished: and that if St. Paul should walk into the great court of Christ Church, or dare to invade the precincts of Balliol, in such guise as he probably presented after one of his weary journeys, he would be cast out as an obtrusive mendicant, and committed to the custody of a policeman. It was true that he would probably find something to say which would startle his delicate reprovers; and it was shocking to think that he might even be tempted to call the Master of Balliol a "whited wall." He sometimes used language of that sort, in spite of his defective toilette, and got into trouble in consequence. Again, St. John the Baptist was not a "well-dressed man." Yet of all that were born of woman "none was greater than he." What did Mr. Kidds suppose would be the fate of that great Preacher of the Desert, if he presented himself at the door of any Episcopal palace in England? Hardly would he be suffered to approach the majestic presence of "My Lord," much less of the ladies of his household; and if, through the compliance of an awe-struck menial, he crossed the solemn threshold, it would only be to hear the justly-offended bishop cry aloud to him from the top of his palatial staircase: "Go away, sir, and never presume to present yourself here again in that disgusting attire."

Well, there had been Baptists in every age, though of a less lofty stature, and the Franciscans were among the present heirs of the great Preacher of the Desert. Had he any representatives in the Anglican Church? He would consent to receive the answer from Mr. Kidds.

DR. VIEWY must express his deep regret that Mr. Benedict and Mr. Kidds had introduced a new and painful element in their debate, by attempting to establish a contrast between the English and the foreign clergy. He thought such personalities imprudent; because, no doubt, if Protestant clergymen could know what the Roman clergy thought of *them*, they would not feel exhilarated by the information. As an illustration of this truth he would repeat, for the benefit of Mr. Benedict and Mr. Kidds, a description of the High-Church clergy it had been his fate to overhear, some months ago, while travelling in a railway carriage on the continent. Two Roman Catholic priests, of cultivated mind and manners, were comparing their experiences acquired during a holiday tour, from which they were returning to their work. One of them had been in England, and spoke with warmth of the kindness and the hospitality which he had enjoyed at Oxford and elsewhere. He regretted that he had found but little else that he could praise. What struck him most, he said, about the Anglican clergy, was a singular want of definiteness of character. Their very appearance, modes of speech, and perpetual uncertainty and self-correction, was suggestive of an attempt to play a part for which they had not the necessary gifts. He should not like to judge unkindly, but they had, as a class, a dreadfully unsupernatural look. You were always tempted to think: "These are men who have never received the Sacraments, and in whose face there is no reflection of the Sacramental Presence." (He had made a note of this expression, which, he confessed, he did not exactly comprehend.) In spite of studied gravity, there was literally nothing in them of the Christian priest. They might be moral gentlemen, but no one would take them for priests. He saw a few who wore a kind of Roman collar, and whose *mise-en-scene* deceived you for a moment; but when you came to look more closely, there was a singular consciousness in their expression, a furtive glancing out of the corners of the eyes, which revealed too plainly their anxiety about the success of the disguise. He got so used to this expression in a week or so, that he could detect it in a moment. It had a very droll effect. As to their inner life and sentiments, they seemed divided into two distinctly opposite classes. Both, he believed, were of exemplary morals, but one was as humble as their unfortunate position allowed them to be, and excused their reluctant isolation with a meek sorrow and hesitation which were really touching. The other class displayed a self-complacent conceit, and, he was obliged to add, a spirit of malice, which, in his own experience, was quite without a parallel. Their hatred of the Catholic Church was positively frightful. They appeared to have no fear, no tenderness, and no modesty. He had observed that they would often go out of their way to express their reverence, generally in extravagant and ludicrous terms, for the "Eastern Church," or any of the Oriental sects, and even sometimes for the Nestorians, while the evil spirit within them seemed to torment them violently whenever the Holy See was named, and forced them to display the *pravitas hæreticorum*.

These were men who, if the Church of England perished to-morrow, would invent some new sect of their own, rather than enter the Catholic Church. They could reign as little kings in a sect, and follow their own conceits; whereas, in the Church, they must be content to serve and obey. But this they would never do, for the spirit of obedience was not in them. Though affecting the language of Catholics, they were more inveterately Protestant in feeling and temper than any of their co-religionists. He was inclined to think, however, that the other class was more numerous, and of *their* conversion good hopes might be entertained, though it was inexpressibly sad to see them wasting their lives in various delusions, pursuing shadows as if they were realities, and running the risk of being surprised by death before they had effected their reconciliation with Holy Church.

The conversation, continued Dr. Viewy, lasted nearly an hour; but perhaps he had quoted enough of it to justify his remark that personalities were imprudent, and might provoke an unpleasant retort. He thought, too, that neither Mr. Benedict nor Mr. Kidds could entertain any doubt as to the answer which Roman priests would give to the question proposed by Dr. Easy: "are English Orders human or divine?"

(The company now began to break up. Mr. Benedict, still smiling, excused himself for retiring to his lodgings on the ground that "he had the office of Vespers to recite," by which he was understood to mean that he was going to read the lively Service which begins with "Dearly beloved," and ends with "Lighten our darkness." Dean Primitive and Archdeacon Chasuble walked away in total silence, arm in arm. Several times their lips parted, as if they were going to speak, but they separated at the door of the former, with a warm grasp, but without having exchanged a word. Mr. Kidds stood at the door for several minutes, looking eagerly down the street, apparently desirous to give Mr. Benedict ample time to get well out of sight. Others would have followed, but Dr. Easy proposed to move again to the dining-room, and refresh themselves with something more generous than tea. This put a stop to further defections. The company drew round the fire, and some lighted cigars. The conversation was resumed with fresh animation.)

DR. EASY, who did not smoke, commenced by observing how very droll it was to see two such men as Benedict and Kidds recognised ministers of the same Church. It would be hard to say what they believed in common. As to Benedict, who really seemed a good fellow at the bottom, in spite of his exorbitant vanity and self-confidence, he would venture a wager that before six months were over he would either be married, or a Catholic,—or relapse into the ordinary routine of English clerical life. The atmosphere of their National Church would soon prove fatal to monkery. Protestant sisterhoods might live and thrive in it, just as they did in Lutheran Prussia, because women would always worship the spiritual guides whom they chose for themselves, and consent to be ruled by them. The very generosity of their nature exposed them, as St. Paul seemed to intimate, to be "led captive" in this way. He had heard without surprise, that the Catholic bishops, who displayed in many things marvellous good sense, never suffered religious communities to choose their own chaplains, and always changed the latter every two or three years. He had no doubt this was a wise precaution. But whether Benedict consoled himself with matrimony or not, poor Kidds, unfortunately for his own peace, was already married, and his wife was such a shrew, that he could not comprehend his enthusiasm about nuptial joys, unless it was a pious fiction designed to soothe his irritable spouse. Primitive and Chasuble, he was afraid, had passed an unpleasant evening, but they would probably get up in the morning none the worse for it. The oddest thing about them, and others of their class, was that they seemed to exult in their regrets and to revel in their miseries. Yet if they believed what they professed, and he was sure they thought they did, they ought to be crushed under the weight of their own convictions; but there was a placidity about their perennial lamentations which made one suspect that their trials were a luxury which they would be sorry to part with. What puzzled him most about them was this, that while they abhorred what the Reformers *taught*, none of the clergy accepted more cordially what they *did*. Even Kidds, poor foolish ranter as he was, could give them a lesson in consistency. So could their predecessors, in the comparatively moderate High-Church schools, which had existed, on a much smaller scale, at former periods. The learned Bramhall warmly protested that he did not "unchurch" the Swiss and German communities, so little sympathy had he with the modern Puseyite doctrine. There was probably not a single writer in the first hundred years of Anglican history who had not, in equally decisive terms, identified himself with the work of the continental Protestants, in spite of occasional protests of a very mild character, which had no meaning, and were not intended to have any. Long after, Reginald Heber, one of their most respected prelates, used officially the same language, and even made a sort of public boast that he had received communion from the Lutheran clergy, and was ready to do so again whenever the opportunity offered. The most conspicuous High-Churchmen whom their community had produced,—even such men as Laud, Leslie, Thorndike, and others,—never, he believed, said anything against the work or hostile to the persons of the Reformers. Their principles did not require it. It was reserved for men of their own day, pressed by the exigencies of their theory, either openly to revile the founders of their Church, or quietly to ignore them. Yet it was hard to see how theologians whose own teaching, as the Puseyites were obliged to maintain, was a tissue of heresies, could found a new branch of the Catholic Church, or claim to be the heirs of the Catholic priesthood. Either the Reformers were doctors and evangelists, and derived their orders and their mission directly from heaven; or they were impostors and heresiarchs, who merited the pillory rather than a "Martyrs' Memorial."

DEAN PLIABLE did not think, with deference to his friend, that they were either one or the other. They were simply men of great vigour and energy, ridding themselves slowly, from the nature of the case, of previous errors, and adopting finally certain opinions according to the influences brought to bear upon them, and even the accident of local circumstance. Bucer had probably more to do with the ultimate shape of Anglican doctrine than all the English Reformers together; and as to the question of Orders, their own language proved how little importance they attached to it. It was a mere chance that they finally adopted, on any point, one set of views rather than another. They would probably have been Presbyterians, if they could have followed their own convictions; but no Tudor would have tolerated such a form of discipline, and the monarchial feeling of the country was opposed to it. There was a time when they would have retained Mass, and then a time when they would have regarded the Eucharist just as the Calvinists did. Cranmer changed his creed half-a-dozen times, and he doubted whether any of the Reformers, after the death of Henry, knew certainly what his own opinions were, or in what direction he was drifting. They were men, and made the mistakes of men; but their mistakes had made England what she was, and freed her from the trammels of ecclesiastical Christianity. It was childish to see in the Reformation anything but a purely human event, but it was one of vast magnitude in its effects upon the destinies of mankind; and he, for one, was willing to accept its benefits, without scanning too critically the character or the motive of the agents to whom they owed them. No one asked, or cared to know, what was the private life, much less the private opinions, of a statesman who introduced a good bill into Parliament. The Reformers did not probably augment the sum of virtue in the world, and might even have too rudely crushed the ecclesiastical and sacramental machinery by which it had for ages been fostered; but they were apostles of freedom rather than of virtue, and having done well what they aimed at, were not to be blamed if they failed to do what was hardly their immediate object. Erasmus and others complained that there was a sensible decay of morals after the introduction of Protestantism; but, it must be remembered in fairness, that men had just cut themselves loose from a vast number of artificial, but potent restraints, and emptied their minds of ideas and principles which had been lodged there from infancy. They might well feel a little light-headed at first. They had flung out their ballast, and were navigating an unknown sea without compass or rudder. The whole process was as purely human as that by which Magna Charta was won, or trial by jury, or the right of self-taxation, or the suppression of the Corn Laws, or a sanitary bill, or a new system of sewerage; but this did not diminish the value of its results. It was absurd to see anything "divine" in it, from first to last, and that which was not divine in its origin could not be so in its effects. He differed as widely from Kidds as from Chasuble; he neither respected the Reformers as prophets, nor defamed them as heretics. They were men, neither much better nor much worse than other men, who began a great work without quite knowing what they were going to do, and who were led, not by angels, but sometimes by princes who would not be disobeyed, sometimes by accident, and most often by one another. It was hard to say what some of them really believed; probably they did not know themselves; but of one thing he was quite certain, that in the whole number there was not one who would not frankly have admitted, what had been abundantly proved in the discussion of that evening, that English Orders were purely human.

THE PROFESSOR OF THEOLOGY, throwing the end of his cigar into the fire, said that it would be a great convenience to all who held office in the English Church, if the candour and good sense of their friend Pliable were a little more common. He knew something personally of the excessive awkwardness of trying to import, for the sake of appearance, a quasi-divine element into a human subject. Whenever he found himself in presence of his class, composed invariably of the same materials,—the majority being profoundly indifferent to theology in general, while a few cherished faintly certain Catholic ideas, which they had picked up in books, and of which he was obliged to take account,—he wished that the University, in appointing a Professor of Anglican Theology, had not thought it unnecessary to say what Anglican Theology was. Let them suppose a body of students, such as was to be found in any Anglican lecture-room whatever, whose theological conceptions ranged, to use a mathematical figure, from a point to a parabolic curve, and whose notions of Christianity,—moral, doctrinal, and historical,—were as various and many-coloured as the patterns of their waistcoats. In front of this motley group stood a gentleman who was assumed to have made up his mind, more or less definitely as to his own views of religion, and who received a liberal salary to impart them to others. He could not conceive an object more worthy of sympathy than the Professor in question. All these young men, the future ministers of their National Church,—some because it was likely to prove a lucrative profession, a few from a certain softness of character which was akin to piety, many because their parents wished it, and more because they were too stupid to be trusted in any other career,—had already received, without knowing it, a sort of theological training. They took with them to college the views of their parents, or of the clique in which they had lived, or of the clergyman who was looked up to by their mothers and sisters. These various ideas,—which they held more firmly in proportion to their ignorance,—they naturally brought with them to the lecture-room; and it was on such tablets as these that the Professor was to write, if he could, a compendium of Anglican Theology. He was to be precise where precision was impossible, dogmatical where every dogma was a subject of dispute, clear where his own Church had purposely left everything in doubt, and peremptory where even the raw youths before him knew that his immediate predecessor had been equally resolute in the opposite sense.

It had happened to him to be present on one occasion at a theological lecture in a great Roman Catholic college. The professor of the day had become his friend, in consequence of a common taste for geology. What struck him about the lecture was its marvellous definiteness. The man seemed to feel that he had the great living Church at his side, and the whole company of heaven at his back. And the attitude of the students was quite as remarkable. There was no more hesitation on their part than on his. One conviction ruled all those free but various intellects. It was a memorable illustration of that state of society which Christianity was destined to form—and seemed to have permanently formed in one communion—in which men of many gifts and diverse races were to be "*of one heart and one mind.*" He found himself envying that fortunate professor, and thought of his own pupils with anything but cheerful feelings.

During the term which followed shortly after the incident referred to, it was recalled to his memory in an unpleasant way. He had been lecturing some freshmen on the subject of Anglican Orders. At the close of the lecture he proposed this question to be answered in writing: "Point out the relations which exist between Holy Order and the rites of Baptism and Confirmation." A young Irishman of great ability, who, a few months later, became a Roman Catholic, and had since distinguished himself at the bar, gave in the following paper, which he had kept as a curiosity to the present day:—

"Privy Council has decided that Baptism may either be, or *not* be, the sacrament of regeneration. The Bishop of Gloucester has officially declared that this decision has been accepted by the English Church. Suppose, then, that one of our bishops should happen to have missed being regenerated in Baptism, has the Church of England made any provision by which the want might be supplied in after life? Could the future bishop contrive to be regenerated in any other way? Would Confirmation supply the defect? Confirmation, the Church of England replies, is *not a sacrament*, but only 'a corrupt following of the apostles.'"

ARCHDEACON JOLLY: Just as the present Anglican doctrine of Baptism is "a corrupt following of the Privy Council."

THE PROFESSOR continued to read:

"One chance remained for the future Bishop, but still, by hypothesis, unregenerate pagan. He had got no touch of Sacramental grace from Baptism or Confirmation, but perhaps Ordination would take the place of both, and imposition of episcopal hands fill his heathen soul with celestial life? This seemed unlikely. The ordaining bishop might happen to be quite as unregenerate as himself; and even if he were not, the English Church declares of Holy Order, as of Confirmation, 'it is *not a sacrament*,' and therefore cannot confer sacramental grace, but is a purely human ceremony, conveying nothing whatever but a license to preach, and the honorary title of Reverend. So that, by the joint testimony of the Articles and the Privy Council, of the Prayer-Book and its authorised expounder, a man might come at length to be a bishop, and indeed was pretty sure to do so, who had never received a Christian sacrament, and would remain to the end of his life 'a child of wrath' in lawn sleeves, with a palace, a peerage, and five thousand a year."

This caustic but humorous freshman added other equally ingenious observations, with which he would not trouble them, and his composition terminated as follows: "What kind of fact, then, does the *Times* or the *Morning Post* design to communicate to the public; when it contains such an announcement as this: 'On Sunday last the following gentlemen were ordained priests by the Lord Bishop of Southampton?' Evidently the meaning was: 'The gentlemen enumerated below, who were probably not regenerate in baptism, certainly not regenerate in confirmation, and therefore most likely never regenerate at all, have received ordination, which itself is only a corrupt following of the apostles, from a bishop who is in precisely the same condition as themselves.'"

His friends would not expect him, continued the Professor, to refute the theological conclusions of this lively undergraduate, nor perhaps consider that it would be very easy to do so. The young man called upon him just before he was received into the Roman Church, and the subject of Orders happened to turn up again in their farewell conversation. He was always remarkable for putting things in a pointed way, and as he (the Professor) admitted that English Orders could not possibly be divine unless they were absolutely identical with Roman, the acute Irishman instantly drew the inevitable conclusion in the following words: " Anglican Orders, whatever else they may be, cannot possibly be the same with Roman, as the Anglican Church must always be eager to maintain; for how can a Church which formally *denies* that ordination is a sacrament either pretend or desire to possess *Roman* Orders, which the Roman Church affirms *to be* a sacrament?"

ARCHDEACON JOLLY, who appeared to be greatly diverted by the Professor's anecdote, thought the latter might have replied to his Irish friend, *rem acu tetigisti*. They were certainly indebted to him for his contribution to the subject of English Orders. As to his argument about an "unregenerate clergy," it was only formidable to those who believed that grace was imparted mainly through sacraments. If that opinion were tenable, then, indeed, there might be good reason for thinking that the National Church was to a large extent a heathen, or at least an unregenerate community. Perhaps it really was so, though the time had not yet arrived when they could all venture to use the plainness of speech which they could employ in their private discussions. But it was evidently coming fast. Two great movements were in progress within the English Church, both introduced and directed by leading members of the clergy, and each carrying away in its swift current the flower of the educated laity. One tended towards Humanism, the other towards Mysticism. One subjected religion to the test of reason, the other forbade reason to dogmatise within the domain of faith. One was in the direction of Rationalism, the other of Popery. These two currents were now running with such a full tide, that philosophical observers need only sit down on the bank and wait for the end.

At such a moment it might be interesting to take a retrospective view of their Church, and of its different schools and parties, some of which were already tending to extinction, others in various stages of decay, and a few preparing to assume new forms which would be developed during the present generation. They might consider them in their representative types, and this he now proposed to do. Many years ago, while he was a curate in a great city, he had enjoyed rare opportunities of studying the amazing variety of clerical types to be found in their community. Even in his youth their constant dissensions had begun to excite remark, and to prepare the way for the general confusion of thought which had since prevailed, and the singular religious revolution now in progress, of which it was impossible to foresee the end; but of which the clergy were themselves the sole cause. He had amused his leisure hours by an attempt to depict these various types, with each of which he was personally familiar. The night was advancing, and their conversation had been unusually protracted, but nobody seemed to be weary, and he should still have time to give at least the substance of a few of the sketches referred to. His friends would say whether they had the merit of being faithful portraits, and whether they threw any light on the subject of that evening's discussion. They had asked themselves whether English Orders were human or divine, and whoever was desirous to maintain the latter hypothesis, —an ambition which he must entirely disclaim,—would admit that *uniformity* of religious belief and *identity* of ecclesiastical character were inseparable parts of that idea. A common divine vocation, accompanied by special gifts for a special object, must necessarily create, as it had actually done in the vast Roman communion, an order of men moulded exactly according to the same type, teaching everywhere the same truths, and ruling their thoughts and lives by the same standard. A divine vocation implied all this, and evidently did not, and could not exist, where these sure tokens of its presence were utterly wanting. Let them consider then whether the infinite *variety* of clerical types in their own community, of which he was about to give a few specimens, could possibly co-exist with the hypothesis of a *divine* vocation.

(The clergy here disposed themselves in attitudes of easy attention, and appeared to feel assured that if the Archdeacon was about to prolong the sitting, they would have no reason for regretting that the moment of departure was delayed. Having referred to some notes which he held in his hand, he proceeded as follows.)

THE HIGH AND DRY CLERGYMAN. His own Rector was the subject of his first sketch. He was the cousin of a cabinet minister, and was a conspicuous member of what had since been called the "*High and Dry*" school. As far as it was possible to attribute to him any fixed religion at all, "salvation by scholarship alone" might be said to be his sole dogmatical conviction. He taught his flock religion as if it were one of the dead languages, but a necessary part of a gentleman's education. He published, on the average, one book every year, of suffocating aridity, and with such titles as the following: "The Church of Rome Convicted of Schism since the reign of Queen Elizabeth; "A new Defence of the Thirty-Nine Articles," which he seemed to think were always in need of fresh defence; "Union with the State, the Duty of the Church;" "Reasons for not joining the Society for the Suppression of Rich Benefices;" and many more equally profitable to mankind, if it had only been possible to read them. His church was frequented by the educated and well-dressed; the few poor, who were all pensioners on the parish bounties, being stowed away under the gallery, whence they could usefully contemplate, with humble respect, the religion of their superiors. In his sermons, which he was constantly printing, on the purely imaginary pretext that somebody had asked him to do so, he treated religion as an anatomical lecturer treats the human body, dissecting it with scientific precision, but always on the assumption that the soul had fled. Indeed, he seemed to him, sitting below in the reading-desk, as if he were trying to persuade himself that he had a religion, but could not succeed in doing so. His object appeared to be to strip religion of all charm, and deprive it of all interest, in which he was uniformly successful. The cruelty of this method towards the women and children of the congregation filled his own mind with a vehement indignation towards his rector, which he was not always able to conceal. One felt in his church— which as little reflected either God or Nature as the fossil resembles the green leaf or the gay insect that waved or fluttered before the flood, —as in a huge mourning coach, in which Truth, Hope and Peace were being carted to a common grave. The only visible purpose of his ministrations was to keep the soul at its greatest possible distance from God; and the only conviction with which he impressed his hearers was, that the Creator had gone to sleep, and that the primary duty of the creature was not to wake Him up.

THE GOOD AND EASY CLERGYMAN was a more agreeable type, and one which he had frequent opportunities of studying. One of this school was incumbent of a large and fashionable chapel, not half a mile from his own parish church. His voice and manner were so tender that he seemed to be always on the point of making everybody an offer of marriage. His life appeared to glide away in a mild and amiable conflict between the claims of piety and good breeding. Sometimes his eye would kindle, and you would have said he was going to launch a rebuke against some popular sin, but good taste came promptly to the rescue, and the sinner's sensibility was gently spared. His sermons were generally a tender panegyric of the natural virtues. He considered them in every aspect, and drew such ravishing pictures of the "devoted mother," or "the Christian at home," or "the good parent's reward," that people said his sermons were as good as a novel, and so they were. He was quite sure he never once alluded to hell during his whole career,— the poor man was dead now,—and people came from all parts of the town to hear him. He had never heard him but once, and was bound to say that it was not unpleasant while it lasted, which was about an hour and a quarter. He was said to make £1500 a year by his pew rents. He satisfied the living members of his flock that they had "found the Lord," or might do so whenever they pleased; and as to the dead ones, he canonized them as soon as the breath was out of them with a facility which would have scandalised the Sacred College at Rome; while it had this advantage over their more cautious methods of procedure, that where *everybody* went straight to Heaven as a matter of course, there could be no need to hear witnesses, and no necessity to make invidious distinctions. He had also his own system of "Indulgences," which did not resemble the Roman one, and of which his treasury was so full, that it almost seemed improvident and ungrateful not to sin, in order to have the pleasure of enjoying them. He discouraged every allusion to doctrine, as not tending to edification, but rather productive of unprofitable controversy, hurtful to that placid composure of spirit which he considered the *summum bonum* of the Christian dispensation. What could it matter whether Baptism was necessary to regeneration, or the Apostolical Succession a poetical myth, so that, as he often observed, you preserved "a calm mind," and were charitable and tolerant of the views of others? His idea of the Almighty seemed to be that He was the author of pure taste and refined breeding, and sin and suffering were the bad manners which marred the harmony of good society. For this reason chiefly it would be very desirable, if possible, to get rid of sin. The Fall, of which he rarely spoke,—for how could such a congregation as his, most of whom came to church in their carriages, be supposed to have fallen? —he appeared to think had been followed by no results to speak of, unless it were the emancipation of the human family from the restraints of a life too exclusively spiritual, bequeathing to Adam's posterity no graver hardship than that of paying more attention to artificial clothing than the simple state of society in Paradise required. As to the final judgment, he seemed to possess some secret which deprived it of all its terrors; and as to the Judge, he evidently regarded Him as the benevolent proprietor of a celestial hotel, "replete with every comfort," into which all well-dressed travellers would be admitted as a matter of course, and where they might expect to enjoy the best society for endless ages.

THE AMATORY PARSON, whose vocation, if he had one, was very human indeed, had a great many representatives. One of his fellow curates, whose father was a half-pay naval officer, belonged to this class. The Rector never allowed him to preach except in the afternoon, because that was the least frequented of the three Sunday services. He was always engaged, or said to be engaged, to some pink or blue bonnet in the flock, though he ultimately left without having justified the rumour. The bonnet in question was conspicuous within easy view of the pulpit every Sunday afternoon. He was a good-looking fellow, but inconceivably shallow and ignorant. If English Orders were ever "divine," they must have ceased to be so before poor Horatio White was ordained. It was really curious to see the air with which the handsome booby mounted the pulpit, drew off his gloves, arranged his pocket handkerchief upon the velvet cushion, satisfied himself by a rapid glance as to the position of the bonnet, and then covered his face to pray. What he prayed for, it would be indiscreet to inquire. His sermons might be described as a botanical effort, so full were they of floral imagery, suggesting the idea that the surest way to Heaven was to cultivate a garden in a wood, by the side of a rippling stream, and to sing in it by moonlight. His favourite subject was Heaven, which he represented as a superior sort of Chiswick or Chatsworth. He appeared to have been there. He evidently knew all about it, but it was rather singular that he never once made the slightest allusion to God. There was a great deal about the Angels, but much more about men and women whom they had known, and the extreme gratification of meeting them again under such agreeable circumstances. His notion of Heaven seemed to be that it was a sort of eternal pic-nic. The poor fellow afterwards married an old woman with money, who led him a dreadful life. He had known several "Amatory Parsons" who came to the same end.

THE CALVINISTIC CLERGYMAN was a very common type when he was a young man, and might be met with even now in almost every large town, and not unfrequently in country villages. He should never forget the Reverend Peter Green,—he might mention his name, for he had gone long since to the Antipodes, where he had become a dignitary,—who was a curate in a church where he sometimes preached at the request of the Rector. The characteristics of Mr. Green's religion were gloom and ferocity. He used the holiest names and truths as if they were stones with which to pelt his congregation. He looked as if he was always on the point of destroying mankind at a single blow, and rather admired his own clemency for not doing it. The habitual tone of his mind towards the Deity, had he expressed it in a prayer, would have required the use of some such language as this: "You and I take precisely the same view of these unregenerate sinners, but we will strive to have patience with them, and if they finally refuse to hear us, we will condemn them to eternal tortures." If he could possibly have admitted the wild suspicion that "Jehovah," the title by which he always called Almighty God, differed from himself on any point of doctrine, he would have regretted it—on Jehovah's account. He seemed to be possessed by a notion that he had personally assisted at the creation of the world, as well as at the founding of Christianity. His sermons were almost invariably about "Paul," and it was very remarkable that though he talked, often in a coarse rude way, about the *work* of the Saviour, he very rarely alluded to his *Person*. He seemed to exist in his mind only as the representative of a particular group of doctrines. The man evidently thought much more of his own wretched opinions than of the Teacher from whom he professed to derive them. He was particularly given to expatiate on the woes of Korazin and Bethsaida, and almost became cheerful in anticipating the fate of their inhabitants. He spoke of the Day of Judgment as if he had been privately consulted about the arrangements to be adopted at that ceremony, and appeared to feel that his own chief enjoyment would consist in hearing the sentence of reprobation pronounced upon the vast majority of mankind. As he did not seem to believe many of the doctrines which are supposed to be taught by the English Church, and openly scoffed at Episcopal Ordination, he was sometimes tempted to wonder why he did not become a dissenter; but he probably felt, like a good many other Anglican clergymen, that it was more convenient to be a dissenter in the Church of England than out of it. He had once the misfortune to hear him preach on a Communion Sunday, and was much struck by the address which he delivered to the intending communicants. His whole anxiety appeared to be to warn them against expecting any possible benefit from it. He said nothing of any kind of benediction which they might reasonably hope to derive from it, but was vehement against the purely imaginary blessings which he warned them *not* to expect. In this, however, he resembled many other classes of the clergy, who habitually preach against the use of this rite, even while supposing that they are preaching in favor of it. In short, there was such a well of bitterness in this man's dark and cruel theology, that all the honey of the religion of Christ turned to gall upon his tongue. The young disliked and feared him, and learned by degrees to shrink from all piety, as if it were something loathsome; but there were certain women of middle age, chiefly disappointed spinsters or soured widows, who adopted his ferocious creed, and became as repulsive and unchristian as himself. If there was anything *divine* in English Orders, they could hardly generate such a teacher as this; and there was perhaps no more decisive argument against that foolish theory, than that their Church had produced, during many successive generations, a multitude of such ministers, and even formed whole classes of Anglican society on the same revolting type.

THE EVANGELICAL CLERGYMAN,—of which class there were two distinct varieties, which took respectively Luther and

Melancthon for their model,—had been very useful in their Church, at a time when the rest of the clergy were of no sort of use whatever. It was almost to be regretted that they were being gradually superseded,—at least as respected their influence on the nation,—by newer and more energetic schools. For many years they, and they alone, had kept alive whatever religious feeling existed in the Church of England. This was a service which should never be forgotten. Before Puseyism was, and while the nation was still slumbering after the horrible stagnation of the seventeenth and eighteenth centuries, the men of this school revived the grand but almost obliterated ideas of a Personal God, of intimate relations between each soul of man and the Divine Redeemer, of a religion of love and willing obedience. All honour to them! They had preached great truths to a people lying in darkness, and no one could say that they had preached wholly in vain. Why, then, had they lost their power and pre-eminence, so that teachers of quite other views were everywhere contending with them, and almost everywhere with success? It seemed to him that this declension was to be attributed to the intellectual feebleness of their system, and its total neglect both of logic and history. Much which they taught was true, but it was only part of the truth; and as they appealed more to feeling and emotion than to either faith or reason,—the first of which they confounded with mere religious sensibility, and the second they scandalized by their private and arbitrary interpretations of Scripture,—they began to fail the moment they ceased to be the *only* earnest men in the nation. They were, moreover, so delightfully unconscious that there were any other inhabitants of Christendom but themselves, and refused with so much simplicity to take any account of Latin, Greek, or Oriental versions of Christianity, that when the so-called "Catholic movement" began a few years ago, and a sudden flood of light was poured into the caves and corners in which they hoped to dwell alone forever, they were amazed to find that while other men could discern perfectly well the objects around them, *they* were only blinded by this unexpected influx of luminous fluid. In this state of imperfect vision, they naturally made many mistakes, stumbled rather than walked, sometimes fell all their length on the ground, and finished by becoming extremely ridiculous. When they were asked what were their relations to the rest of the great Christian family, they claimed kindred with all sorts of discreditable ancestors,—obscene

Lollards, and noisy Wickliffites, and unbelieving Waldenses,—and so fell into shame, and gave their adversaries an easy victory. He was sorry to say it, but they were dreadfully narrow-minded, and had so little grasp of the great doctrine of Christian fraternity, that they wished to have a Gospel, a Church, and a Heaven all to themselves. The Puseyites,—the best of whom had a rich fund of playfulness and humour,—only laughed at them, and very soon robbed them of such of their disciples as had any mental cultivation. The combat between these two schools was always an *impar congressus*, and the Evangelicals went to the wall. They still existed in great numbers; and Mr. Bennet had lately insisted, with perfect truth, though in contempt of his own principles, that they had as good a right to teach in the English Church as their successful rivals; but they had fallen on evil days, and their brief season of triumph and authority had faded away never to return.

THE RITUALISTIC CLERGYMAN was a plant of recent growth in their Church, but had quickly arrived at maturity. Whether it would display a hardy nature, or be shrivelled, like other tender shoots, by the first frost, or beaten to the earth by the first thunder-shower, a little time would probably show. Meanwhile, it was not difficult to account for its appearance. The unadorned Anglican service, as they might venture to confess among themselves, since their congregations had long ago made the same discovery, was a little dreary. No one would think of describing it as a lively way of spending a couple of hours. People in church always looked as if they had come with an honest English resolve to get through an unpleasant duty. They had made up their minds to face it, and the determination did them credit. But they generally went home again with a deep sense of relief. They had done their duty, but were heartily glad it was over. He had heard that in New York, many of the best seats in the numerous Catholic churches were invariably rented by wealthy Protestants, not because they had any active preference for Catholic doctrine, but solely because they found the service less dismal than their own. In England, there was still too much dislike to Popery to allow of such a diversion. Yet it had become urgent to do something to diminish the patient suffering of their flocks. The humbler classes, it was true, could sleep, and they used the privilege; but a sense of personal dignity denied this solace to the upper ranks. At length the Ritualists came to their relief.

It was a new fact in their history, that for some time past people had actually found pleasure in going to Church! And they went there willingly, no longer tempted by the languid excitement of criticising the preacher, in whom they now felt very little interest. They had found something more attractive. Cheerful music borrowed for the most part from Catholic sources, had supplanted the dreary psalm tunes which nourished their gloomy youth. Choral singing, bright and animated, banished all desire to sleep. Gay flowers adorned the renovated temple, which of old had oppressed and chilled the senses like a huge family vault. Surplices had become of snowy whiteness and unfamiliar shapes, and stoles of strange dimensions and unwonted hues, lent a new grace to the ministrants. The communion table had become an "altar," and even long extinguished candles had burst into light. Instead of a solitary cleric, of unimpressive aspect, who looked as if he had just left a more agreeable scene and would be glad to get back to it, a decorous procession of comely youths preceded the ministers, who contrived to be as numerous as possible, and carefully avoiding the lax gestures and unmortified looks of the cathedral clergy, moved with studied gravity to their appointed seats, amid the loud pealing of the organ. It was evident that care and forethought had presided at these arrangements, and while a certain expression in the faces of the clergy appeared to say to the congregation,—"We flatter ourselves, this will meet with your approval;" a cheerful look of contentment seemed to respond for the people,—"You deserve it, for you have relieved our Sunday of half its gloom."

If the Ritualists had been content with this peaceful success, they would have been hailed, at least by the educated classes, as benefactors, and they would have deserved the title. It was surely no mean triumph to have made the English Sunday almost tolerable. But it soon became apparent that they had other objects in view. It was no longer enough that the surplice should be of unspotted purity, unless it were also covered with a decorated vestment, familiar in Catholic churches but utterly unknown in their own, of which the fashion and colour varied with the feast, and symbolised, to discerning eyes, the Saint, the Virgin, or the Martyr of the day. The "altar," too, must now be approached with bended knee, because it was no longer the seat of the simple and homely rite which had contented their uninstructed fathers, but of "Tremendous Mysterys" and an "August Sacrifice." Censers of gold or silver must lend their aid, and waft clouds of incense through choir and nave, which for three centuries had been perfumed with meaner odours. And doctrine kept pace with ritual, or rather outstripped it. The people were now told that the Real Presence was the central object of Christian devotion, the Daily Sacrifice the highest expression of Christian worship. Sacramental confession was the surest remedy for sin in this world, and the safest pledge of forgiveness in the next. Protestantism was an abomination, and the English nation was assured that it had always been Catholic without knowing it. The Reformation was a trifling historical incident, of hardly any real importance, and the best thing they could do was to forget it. The Church, by her own nature, was incapable of error; but as she had unfortunately been under a cloud for a good many centuries, a few English clergymen had undertaken to perform her functions until further notice. Such were the principal chapters of the new Ritualistic catechism.

A certain number of hearers approved these ideas as true in themselves, without pausing to consider in what place they heard them, or by what lips they were uttered. But a far larger number vehemently declined to embrace them. The latter might be divided into three classes. The first only laughed, and thought the whole affair an indifferent comedy, played by actors who had not learned their parts. The second were indignant, threw dust into the air, and talked about "treason against the Church of England." The third, more thoughtful and judicious, took a deeper view of the whole subject, and replied to the Ritualists in such terms as the following:

"The doctrines which you teach are either true or false. On the latter hypothesis they need not be discussed; but if you can prove them to be true, you will have proved, at the same time, that the Church of England is the most guilty of all Christian communities. You affirm that they are divine, and *therefore* necessary to salvation; yet many successive generations of men, taught by the English Church or her appointed ministers, lived and died in utter ignorance of them, knowing only that by her formularies, and by the mouths of her bishops and clergy, she had mocked and derided them, and taught the whole nation to do the same. They may be true in themselves, as you insist; but if they are, the Church of England, as you cannot refuse to admit, is a synagogue of Satan, and most of her members are now, and ever have been, in foul heresy and in the shadow of death.

"So much for the effect of your new teaching on the Church to which you profess to belong; let us next consider it in relation to yourselves. If your doctrines are true, as you assert, why do we find you patiently continuing in a Church which has permitted them to be blasphemed in the past, and in daily communion with a clergy who revile them in the present? Do you, or do you not, in the full exercise of your liberty, communicate *in sacris* with men who call that devilish which you call divine? and, if so, in what do you differ from *them*, except in this, that they have the excuse of holding errors which they believe to be true, while you have the infamy of countenancing doctrines which you proclaim to be false? By your own confession, *their* position is at all events better than yours. They are simply heretics without suspecting it, while you refuse to separate from the heresy which you affect to regard with horror. If the Reformation was a disaster, why do you consent to minister in a Church which has always approved it; and if the Catholic theology be true, why do you refuse obedience to the Church which has always taught it? Why are you Catholics in condemning the Church of England, and Protestants in resisting the Church of Rome? Be one thing at a time, and tell us, whether you belong to any Church at all, or whether you believe *yourselves* to be the Church, and that all mankind should learn wisdom from you?"

The Ritualist, who had a right to speak on his own behalf, replied after this manner: "I call myself a Catholic priest, because I am either that or a ridiculous impostor, and I object to be considered in that light. I claim the power of the Keys, because they belong to the priestly office, and I will not allow that the clergy of any other Church have more power than I have. I can consecrate the Host, though I am not quite sure what that means, because I should be only a Protestant minister if I could not, and a Protestant minister is the object of my contempt. I can absolve from sin, though the English clergy never knew they could do it, because the commission was given to somebody, and therefore it must have been given to me. I teach the Church of England what she ought to hold, and instruct the Church of Rome what she ought to retract, because I clearly perceive the deficiencies of the one, and detect the excesses of the other. I assert that my doctrines are part of God's truth, but I communicate with those who flatly deny them, because, when I am taunted with this, I can always reply that it is the mark of a self-willed man to seek another communion in order to quiet his conscience. I countenance, by remaining in the Church of England, all the mortal heresies which have ever existed in her, but I tell my accusers that I only remain in her in order to remove them. I am in communion with no Church in the world, but I invite them all to come into communion with me, and indicate the terms on which I will permit them to do so. I am not in schism, though I dwell in solitude, because the other Christian bodies obstinately refuse to associate with me; and I am not in heresy, though I every day communicate with heretics, because I do it only for their good. I do not obey my bishop, but I propose to him to obey me, which he foolishly declines to do. All Churches have erred, but I am ready to teach them all, if they will only listen to me; and though the perfect idea of Christianity has perished from the earth, I am able to restore it at any moment, whenever I shall be requested to do so. I remain in the Church of England, though she allows most of her clergy to teach lies, because I do not choose to quit her; and I refuse to enter the Church of Rome, though she forces all her priests to teach truth, because I do not choose to obey her. I prefer to obey myself, because I find no other authority worthy to be obeyed; and though I admit that this position has its disadvantages, I must positively decline to exchange it for any other."

THE SENSATIONAL CLERGYMAN, the last on his list, was much more common at the present day than when he was a young man. He was simply a product of the law of supply and demand. He was wanted, and therefore he came into being. All large towns possessed at least one specimen of him, but it was in fashionable watering places that he found his most congenial home. Brighton was his paradise, and he reigned as a king at Leamington and Bath. His sermons were published every Monday morning, and sold for a penny. It was apparently on their titles that the largest amount of thought was expended. They were sometimes as full of delightful and provoking mystery as those of the fashionable novels. Perhaps this was their chief merit, as they generally promised a good deal more than they gave; but you did not find that out till you had paid your penny. He was in the habit even now of cheerfully sacrificing that sum, when he happened to be at the sea-side, not because he cared to read such sermons, but simply for the sake of seeing what some people would accept as spiritual instruction. In that point of view they were curious and instructive.

He remembered on one occasion actually hearing a sermon of this kind at Brighton. He had persuaded a French friend, well known in the literary circles of Paris, to accompany him, though he had some difficulty in doing so. The preacher was always famous for his oratorical successes, and the rapt attention of the audience proved that, at least in their opinion, he fully deserved his reputation. "*Qu' en pensez vous?*" he said to his friend, as they walked away together from church. "*Vous m' avez joué un mauvais tour,*" was the prompt reply; "*c' était d' un imbécile incroyable.*"

The sole design of the "sensational" clergy was evidently to present religious truths, or what they considered to be such, in a startling and unexpected form. They seemed to have no higher purpose than to make the public talk, first about their sermons, and then about themselves. And it was not to be denied that they "had their reward." If people once came to like such sermons, it seemed to him in the nature of things that they should like them more and more. The only difficulty, as in so many other cases, must lie in the first step. No one knew this better than the preacher himself. If the congregation once took his bait, he was too skilful an angler to let the fish escape. The very air with which he launched his net showed his confidence in his own art. The moment he mounted his pulpit, and cast a glance over the shallow sea below him, the incubus of his huge conceit fell upon you like a weight. He knew, indeed, how to assume an expression of elaborate humility, but the mask was transparent to all save those who were under the spell, and came only to admire. To others he was inexpressibly diverting, though a few minutes sufficed to exhaust the entertainment. If he had ever taught the Catechism,—which he would have disdained to do,—he would have comprehended it all in one question and answer. "How many sacraments are there?"—"*One* only as indispensably requisite to salvation, and that is to listen to Me." And for this reason, because he claimed the whole undivided homage of his congregation, he nourished an almost savage hatred against Ritualists of every school. They were his only formidable rivals. Sacraments, Ritual, and choral singing, were but odious accessories of religion, which presumed to intrude their offensive attractions between him and his admirers. A sensational preacher at Liverpool began a sermon, a few years ago, in a church which was not his own, by a vigorous *extempore* assault upon the choral service just concluded. He evidently thought it indecent, though he gave other reasons for his displeasure, that "singing men and women" should divide with *him* the interest of the congregation.

He (Archdeacon Jolly) had frequently observed, in the course of a career which ran through half a century, that no vanity was so exorbitant and insatiable as clerical vanity. There were, as everybody knew, sincere and modest ministers, who thought much more about their message than about themselves, but he was speaking now of types to whom this praise did not belong. He had been at various times amused or pained by the fatuity of artists, of musicians, of literary men, and of other sensitive and irritable tribes; but he knew no fatuity which could be compared with that of preachers. Perhaps the dangerous peculiarities of their position accounted for the exceptional development of this vice. Other orators spoke, as a rule, to men, and were constrained, as far as their gifts allowed, to speak with sobriety and good sense. But with an audience chiefly female, every one of whom was gazing upon you with two eyes far more eloquent than your own, and disposed to give you credit for all the gifts with which their lively imagination could invest you, a weak and foolish man became inevitably weaker and more foolish. Indeed, he not unfrequently became a mere conceited driveller, and learned to think, and to persuade admiring ladies to agree with him, that the success of Christianity was mainly due to the fact that *he* consented to preach it. Texts of Scripture which a rational being would read on his knees were only used by him to round a sentence, and mysteries of which saints would speak in a whisper were profaned to adorn a climax. The *Saturday Review* had well expressed this fact, though he could only quote the passage from memory. Comparing the English with the continental clergy, it observed that "the latter were too much absorbed in what they preached to have any recollection of themselves, while the former were too much absorbed in themselves to contemplate any higher subject."

It was a natural result of their mode of handling sacred themes, and of constantly talking about their own convictions, that preachers of this class fell far below even the popular standard of religious reverence. Anxious above all things to identify their paltry personality with everything they preached about, and always putting themselves between the truth and the hearers whose view they totally obstructed, these men grew always incurably profane, from the habit of talking lightly and impertinently about things they neither felt nor understood. And yet such persons as these, and numbers of them, who would have ignominiously failed in any other calling than that of preaching to women, were really a power in this country! They might be tracked all round her coasts; for though they contrived to flourish in the denser atmosphere of the capital and of other great cities, they were especially a sea-side plant, and required the culture of feminine hands for their full development, and reached their highest stature in the midst of those languid and otiose populations which seek their recreation by the shores of the great sea. Their names were heralded in the weekly columns of the local papers, along with the fashionable arrivals, the projected entertainments, and other topics of inferior interest. Their hours of preaching were announced as carefully as those of the railway departures. They professed all sorts of creeds, which was a great convenience to the inhabitants, who were thus enabled to cultivate whatever form of religion suited their tastes, while all continued equally attached members of the same National Church. Sometimes it would happen to one of them to be outstripped by his rivals in the race for popularity, and it was curious that, in these cases, they all adopted the same plan for recovering the favour which seemed about to desert them. To announce a new course of sermons against Popery, with large placards displayed in the shop windows, or carried about in the places of public resort, was always a sure resource against impending disgrace. They all had to try it in turns, and it succeeded with all. He once heard the opening sermon of such a series. It was preached by a man who had contrived to obtain a Master's degree at Cambridge, and it lasted exactly one hour and sixteen minutes. It was, of course exclusively on the subject of the Roman Catholic religion, of which the preacher knew simply nothing, but gave an account which would have been absurd and calumnious if he had been describing Buddhism or Mormonism. And yet the man spoke with an affected tenderness and regret, and so melodiously withal, that, although his odious slanders merited only the scourge or the pillory, his hearers evidently thought it an exercise of sweetest charity to prove that the Christians of all past ages, and three-fourths of those now living, were criminals, idiots, and idolaters. Stupid and guilty as the preacher was, his congregation, who gave him their silent applause, were worthy of such a pastor. For his own part, the sermon brought to his recollection some of his Roman Catholic friends, whose opinions he was not able to adopt, but who were as superior to this frothy babbler in intellect and attainments as they were in rational piety and profound conviction.

He would only add, without further details, that he regarded the sensational clergyman as one of the prime religious nuisances of the day, requiring prompt and vigorous suppression, especially on account of the irreparable evil which he wrought on the female mind and character. But the clock had just caught his eye, and warned him to conclude. Many additional types and sub-types of the English clergy would be found among the sketches in his portfolio, but he should weary his friends if, at so late an hour, he attempted to go through the entire series. He would ask their permission to make a single reflection, and so bring his remarks to an end.

They had considered in the debate of that evening, whether English Orders were human or divine; and the discussion had naturally branched into the collateral inquiry, whether the English clergy were Catholic priests or Protestant ministers. The sketches which he had presented were his own contribution to the solution of both these questions. Their Church now numbered, he believed, about sixteen thousand teachers of all classes; and though it would be an exaggeration to affirm that they professed sixteen thousand different religions, it would certainly be difficult, if not impossible, to find any two of them in the same parish who held exactly the same views on even the highest truths of the Christian revelation, while their differences ranged through the whole vast field between Arianism on the one side, and Romanism on the other. If, then, a national clergy, of whom no two could be forced, in any town or village of England, either by free enquiry, or ecclesiastical persuasion, or state authority, to unite in a common belief, and who often differed from one another as widely as the limits of human opinion permitted, were nevertheless recipients of *the same mysterious and constraining grace,* flowing directly from the august rite of ordination, and infused into the soul by a special divine operation, expressly to produce a *uniform* habit of mind and heart, and a *uniform* conception of religious truth; he would simply ask, what must they think of Christianity or of its Author?' Could any supposition be more fatally injurious to either? If the Almighty, in instituting the supernatural rite in question, chiefly that the world might be convinced by the apostolic life and indissoluble unity of its teachers, had only succeeded in creating, as in their own land, a clergy notorious for living just as the world around them lived, and whose perpetual dissensions about the most sacred dogmas of religion were a scandal to themselves, and a stupefaction even to their enemies; he did not see how they could resist the inevitable conclusion, that Christianity was as purely *human* in its nature and results, as its English teachers had ever been in every feature of their lives, and in every characteristic of their ministry.

(The company now left their seats, and gathered in a confused group round Dr. Easy, who had been standing during the previous speech with his back to the fire. Some had already extended their hands to bid him farewell, when he indicated by a sign that he desired to speak.)

DR. EASY said he could not permit his friends to depart, as they now manifested their intention to do, without thanking them both for their attendance on that occasion, and for the part which they had taken in a discussion of great interest and importance. He would not abuse his privilege as their host by adding to the discourse of the Archdeacon more than a few brief words. They had arrived, he supposed, at a common conviction on the two great questions of Authority in the Anglican Church, and the real character of her Orders. It was at once their wisdom and their safety to insist that both were purely human. Any other theory, as the Archdeacon had clearly proved, would expose not only themselves but their common Christianity to contempt and ruin. Either ordination, as it existed in the English Church, was *not* a rite intended to produce a supernatural effect, except in a sense which might with equal justice be applied to the orders of Mr. Spurgeon or Mr. Newman Hall; or, if it *was*, the reformed and Protestant ministry established by Elizabeth and inaugurated by Parker, which had never displayed the faintest trace of any such effect, was a failure so portentous, that they must remain forever silent in the presence of any scoffing infidel who should use it as an argument against the truth of Christianity.

He trusted, therefore, that they were about to separate that night with this practical conclusion, that the idea of a Catholic

Priesthood, one in doctrine and divine in endowments, existing in the English Church, was not only a contradiction of her whole history, but absolutely inconsistent with the belief that Christianity was true. Either that foolish notion must be abandoned, or they must honestly admit that, at least, the English Church was a delusion. For if any man could deliberately maintain, as a small party among them desired to do, that the entire body of the English clergy had been, from the beginning, a supernatural caste, though it was undeniable that they had always exactly resembled the laity in all their habits, principles, and actions; that they had received a special vocation from heaven to teach the same unvarying doctrine, though no two of them could ever agree together what that doctrine was; that they possessed the faculty of retaining or remitting sin, though, for three centuries, they had never once attempted to use it, and had bitterly derided the assumption of it by the clergy of another community; that they were clothed, by the transforming grace of Orders, with angelic purity and virginity, though they and their bishops had ever been even more impatient of a life of continence than any other class of human society; that they were able to call down God upon a human altar, though their own founders began their career by pulling down altars, and their own tribunals ruled that the English Church denied their existence; that the chief function of their ecclesiastial life was to offer the daily sacrifice, though the Church of England had carefully obliterated every trace of that mystery from the national mind; and finally, that the highest spiritual privilege of their flocks was to adore the consecrated Host, though their own Prayer-book expressly declared that such worship was "idolatry to be abhorred of all faithful Christians:" if, he said, any man could seriously affirm the series of propositions here enumerated, and many more like them, he should be ready to admit, what it would no longer be possible to deny, that neither religion nor history had any real meaning, and that modern Christianity had been more fertile in childish conceits and preposterous delusions than any system of heathen mythology with which he was acquainted.

If, on the other hand, they were content to believe with the whole nation, that the English clergy were simply the representatives of the English Reformation; that they were Protestant ministers, not Catholic priests; that they were distinguished in nothing from other men, except as having undertaken to remind them from time to time of truths which all were too apt to forget; they would then assume the only character which really belonged to them, or in which either their own communion or any other would ever consent to recognise them. In that case, they would no longer expose either themselves or their religion to the world's contempt, nor unwittingly furnish the unbeliever with a fatal argument against the truth and the reasonableness of Christianity. The Church of England had never been the home of the Supernatural, as all mankind knew from her own history; and to try to introduce so strange an element into such a receptacle would be a far more dangerous experiment than to "pour new wine into old bottles." They might as well attempt to inclose the lightning which could shiver rocks, in the hands of an infant, as to make the English Church the shrine of mysteries *which she had existed only to deny.*

> (General cheering, which brought the remarks of Dr. Easy to an end; and the company, shortly after, separated.)

www.ingramcontent.com/pod-product-compliance
Lightning Source LLC
Chambersburg PA
CBHW031324160426
43196CB00007B/649